"Those who are winning

are attuned to everything—

the wind, the grass,

the sounds, everything.

It isn't blocking out, it's

taking in. It's being so fully

aware of the moment that

you're protected by it."

Shirley Spork

Today's LPGA players consistently combine an impressive power game with the delicate skills needed for a successful short game. **Preceding page:** *Leslie Spalding* **Above:** *Tina Barrett* **Facing page:** *Akiko Fukushima.*

CHAMPIONS OF WOMEN'S GOLF

CELEBRATING FIFTY YEARS OF THE LPGA

Edited by

NANETTE S. SANSON

QUAILMARK BOOKS LLC

NAPLES, FLORIDA

DEDICATION

This book is dedicated to the memory of

MILDRED "BABE" DIDRIKSON ZAHARIAS.

1911–1956

In many ways, "Babe" typified the American dream. Although

born into poverty to Norwegian immigrant parents, Babe

persevered to become one of the greatest athletes of all time.

Her amateur accomplishments are legendary, culminating in gold

medals for track and field in the 1932 Olympics. Babe played many

sports, excelling in all. Switching to golf, Babe demonstrated the

same dedication, hitting more than a thousand balls in daily

practice. She won 41 professional golf events from 1940-55 and

took home a record-setting 17 straight titles in 1947 as an amateur.

As one of the founders of the LPGA, Babe was tireless in her

support and promotion of the new association during its early years.

In 1999, Sports Illustrated elected Babe Didrikson Zaharias as winner

of the 20th Century Sports Award for women's individual sports.

We salute her.

CREDITS

PUBLISHED BY:
QUAILMARK BOOKS LLC
a division of QuailMark Media Group LLC
4500 Executive Drive
Naples, Florida 34119

PUBLICATION UNDER THE DIRECTION OF:
Nanette S. Sanson, Editor-In-Chief

PHOTOGRAPHY EDITORS:
Deborah A. Levinson
Nanette S. Sanson

TEXT EDITORS:
Sandi Higgs, Fact verification
Julie G. Marvel, Text Editor
Nanette S. Sanson, Captions Editor
Melissa Yow, Copy Editor

AUTHORS:
Melanie Hauser, Five Decades of Champions/The Record Breakers
Liz Kahn, The LPGA Story/LPGA Tour Hall of Fame
Lisa D. Mickey, The LPGA Founders/On Tour/Into The Future

CAPTION TEXT:
Sandi Higgs
Lisa D. Mickey
Nanette S. Sanson

BOOK AND JACKET DESIGN:
Landgraff Design Associates Ltd.

Photo Credits: page 155

Color separations by Bergman Graphics

Printed and bound in Canada by Friesens Corporation

AN LPGA OFFICIALLY LICENSED PRODUCT
For information about the LPGA please contact:
LPGA Headquarters, 100 International Golf Drive, Daytona, FL 32124
Tel.: 904.274.6200 or Website: www.lpga.com

Library of Congress Catalogue Card Number 99-069620

ISBN 0-96776-390-8

This book is available for purchase for business or sales promotional use.
For inquiries regarding the purchase or distribution of this book please contact:
QUAILMARK BOOKS LLC
941.596.2470
nsanson@quailmark.com
www.quailmarkbooks.com

ACKNOWLEDGMENTS

This book owes its life to one angel, Tom Brown, who had the vision and the enthusiasm to take the concept to production. This book owes its successful delivery, in the amazingly short nine months of research and production time, to a small team of very creative, supportive, determined, and patient individuals. From the early adventures into the archives of our photographers' files to this last page of writing, the ongoing participation and encouragement of several contributors made a very special difference in the realization of the project.

For jumping on the band wagon at a moment's notice and staying there through thick and thin, I will be forever indebted to Deborah Levinson, a consummate multitasker and lifesaver. The photography brought the LPGA story to life and I am particularly grateful to Dee Darden and Kim Higgins for responding time and again to special requests. Their spirit and art enabled me to add a touch of heart and magic to many of the pages. If text is the thread that binds the pages, then Lisa D. Mickey is a master weaver. It seemed the more hectic the project became, the more enthusiastic Lisa was to help, contributing text and encouragement whenever needed.

With no time for hesitation, several individuals were always there to fit a wayward piece of the puzzle together. For turning each of my concepts into a cohesive and artistic element of the book, I am indebted to Michael Landgraff. I am ever grateful to Diane Belanger for transforming a multitude of information from every aspect of the project into logical order, Melissa Yow for her wonderful spirit and talent in editing the editors and Anne Brayley for her generous contributions of office space, marketing insight and encouragement throughout the project.

I would also like to recognize and thank several special contributors to the book's content. Mark Emerson Golf of Columbus, Ohio, contributed many of the signatures, which appear on pages 104-105. Charlcie Hopkins of StopAction Sports submitted many of the quotations, which appear throughout the book.

This book would not have been possible without the ongoing support of the LPGA and its staff. In particular, a special thanks to Sandi Higgs and Carol Killian for being so readily available in assisting the progress of our research and fact verification.

Finally, the publisher and editor would like to extend their gratitude to the Mead Corporation, a sponsor of the LPGA, for their contribution to this project. A forest products company, Mead's sponsorship made it possible for us to use Signature Suede, one of their finest papers, in the production of the book, enhancing the color and quality of the product.

Facing page: *Juli Inkster approaches the 18th green at the Japan Airlines Big Apple Classic.*

Right: *As Tammie Green (left) and Liselotte Neumann discovered, the galleries at the du Maurier Classic often include an audience of Canadian geese.*

CONTENTS

49th United States Women's ...
Questions as to the Rules of Golf shall b...

MOCHRIE, Dottie

Competitor   Date

HOLES	1	2	3	4	5	6	7	8	9	
YARDS	470	370	142	377	170	406	367	371		36
PAR	5	4	3	4	3	4	4	4	4	
Round	5	5	②	4	3	4	5	4		

Signature

	10	11	12	13
	351	334	468	204
	④	4	⑤	3
	3	4	4	2

Competitor's Signature
Betsy K...

31ST U.S. WOMEN'S OPEN CHAMPIONSHIP

ADMIT ONE

MAY 27, 1951

WEATHERVANE WOMEN'S OPEN GO... TOURNAMEN...

INTRODUCTION

BY TY M. VOTAW, *LPGA Commissioner*

The year 2000 marks the 50th anniversary of the Ladies Professional Golf Association (LPGA), an association born out of the vision, dreams and determination of 13 courageous women that has evolved into the world's oldest, longest-running women's professional sports organization.

The magnitude of this achievement is hard for many of us to understand. In today's environment of Title IX and equal opportunity for male and female athletes, it is hard to fathom exactly what it took for the fledgling LPGA to get its start and succeed. In 1950, the world was still recovering from World War II, and the focus was on returning life to the way it was before the war and building on the booming prosperity. Sports fans had their sights set on rebuilding the sports franchises in football and baseball, not on establishing a woman's professional golf league. Thank heaven the 13 founders of the LPGA were not easily daunted.

Armed with the burning desire to play professional golf, the willingness to do any and everything to achieve that goal and a passion for golf, these women overcame the odds and built the foundation for what has become the world's pre-eminent women's professional golf tour.

The moxie of Babe Zaharias, the charisma of Patty Berg, the drive of Louise Suggs and the selfless contributions of Alice Bauer, Bettye Danoff, Helen Dettweiler, Marlene Hagge, Helen Hicks, Opal Hill, Betty Jameson, Sally Sessions, Marilynn Smith and Shirley Spork combined to create a "league of their own" that has succeeded. The LPGA would not be the success it is today without their efforts or the millions of fans and friends who have contributed to the LPGA's growth.

The contributions of these 13 women extend far beyond women's golf. They set the stage for women's sports to grow 25 years before tennis star Billie Jean King defeated Bobby Riggs. The need for and establishment of Title IX, which requires equal athletic opportunities for women and men in collegiate sports, can also be traced back to the seeds sowed in the 1950s. Women's sports are enjoying their greatest popularity and prosperity as we move into a new century, and the LPGA founders have a part in this success.

Today, the LPGA boasts a membership of more than 1,500 women golf professionals between its Tournament and its Teaching and Club Professional (T&CP) divisions. The LPGA Tour, which showcases the world's best women golfers week-in and week-out, features more than 40 events and total purses in excess of $36 million. The LPGA T&CP Division is the industry leader in "teaching teachers to teach" and is further recognized for its grassroots golf programs for women and junior players.

I believe the LPGA's success and stature today have exceeded even its founders' wildest dreams. The business of the association has moved from the trunks of cars in the 1950s into a modern, 21,000-square foot headquarters in Daytona Beach, Fla. Through the pages of this book, you will become friends and fans of the individuals who have built the LPGA over the last 50 years . . . a truly remarkable achievement.

The 13 founders of the LPGA could never have imagined that it would become the longest-running women's sport organization in the world.
Preceding Page: *Juli Inkster.* **Facing page:** *Memorabilia from the World Golf Hall of Fame collection.* **Above:** *The Rolex Player of the Year Trophy.*

FOREWORD

BY DAVE ANDERSON, *The New York Times*

While researching an article on Babe Zaharias several years ago, I telephoned Patty Berg for her memories of the LPGA's first dominant golfer.

"Until Babe came along," Patty said, "women were all swing and no hit. Babe swung, but she also hit. She put power into the women's game."

Babe flaunted that power. At clinics, she would belt a big drive, then turn to the gallery and bark, "Don't you men wish you could hit a ball like that?" The men nodded. That power in Babe's tee shots, as well as her finesse around the greens, translated to the power to attract not just women but men and the media to the women's game.

In Babe's time, the sports public and the sports media had grown up with another Babe's power, Babe Ruth's 714 home runs. As golf's Babe won 41 tournaments in her relatively brief career before succumbing to cancer, it was easy for the public and the media to identify her with power and to realize that other LPGA golfers had power too. In a word, they realized that women could play.

Other women soon carried the torch that Babe had lighted. Players such as Patty Berg, Betty Jameson and Louise Suggs, then Mickey Wright, Kathy Whitworth, Betsy Rawls, Carol Mann,

Sandra Haynie and Judy Rankin. Whitworth holds golf's all-time record with 88 tournament victories (Sam Snead's 81 are the most on the men's PGA Tour). And then along came Nancy.

During the men's 1978 United States Open, a prankster tacked a namecard on the media-tent scoreboard that read, "Lopez, Nancy." Next to it were the numbers "3-4-3-3," which would have put Lopez three under par for Cherry Hill's first four holes. The namecard and the numbers were quickly removed as being too frivolous for the Open, but that summer the message was clear: Nancy Lopez had transcended the women's tour.

On the Sunday of that Open won by Andy North, Lopez won her record fifth consecutive tournament, the Bankers Trust Classic in Rochester, N.Y.

Lopez was only 21 then. And this Nancy with the smiling face would endear herself to America's public along with JoAnne Carner, Pat Bradley, Patty Sheehan, Betsy King, Amy Alcott and Juli Inkster, as well as Annika Sorenstam of Sweden, Laura Davies of England, Karrie Webb of Australia and dozens of others.

They are all golf descendants of Babe Zaharias, who, as Patty Berg said, was the first to "put power into the women's game" — power off the tee and power to attract galleries and the media who realized that the women on the LPGA Tour could play.

While the LPGA Tour players draw large crowds and media coverage to each tournament with their skill and talent, they are also recognized for their friendly and generous interaction with the public and the press. **Facing page:** *Laura Davies* **Above:** *Kris Tschetter.*

PREFACE

By BETTY HICKS, *LPGA Pioneer*

My mother told me that with above-average competitive drive and above-average intelligence, you can do practically anything you want.

When I became a professional golfer in 1941 at the age of 21, I needed to remember that advice. We few professionals had to try to make a living, to create from nothing an organization that would carry on into the future. It is important in life to have role models and I was motivated by reading about Babe Didrikson's accomplishments as a track-and-field star in the 1932 Olympics and by seeing the pilot, Amelia Earhart, fly from my local airfield.

When we started the women's tour, we thought of ourselves as enthusiastic pioneers, but we did not have grandiose ideas about what we were doing. We were trying to make a living at something we enjoyed. Occasionally we gave a passing thought that we were creating opportunities for women, but mostly we were trying to overcome the social barriers. We had been raised in an era when young women were supposed to be modest, and that modesty excluded hitting the ball hard, practicing golf or seeking publicity for our tour.

The idea of a professional golf tour for women was triggered in 1943 by the sheer inequality of reward in the Tam O'Shanter tournament in Chicago. Byron Nelson received the winner's check of $14,000; my victory in the same event earned me $500. Our small group decided at that moment that women golfers needed their own professional division.

The Women's Professional Golf Association (WPGA), of which I was the first president, was born in 1944. It was a struggle against the odds in those early years, but it sowed the seeds for the establishment of the LPGA in 1950.

At that time, Fred Corcoran was promoting Babe Didrikson Zaharias and the tour. By 1953, we were an established, but shaky LPGA and were responsible for running the show ourselves — with a group of highly individual characters!

Babe, leading after two rounds in Atlantic City that year, made a disturbing announcement: "I am going into New York City tonight on business. If somebody doesn't raise that $1,200 first-prize money before I leave, I won't bother to come back."

If Babe went, the gate went with her. A gallant club member jumped to the rescue with the offer of a $1,000 bonus for anyone who could total under 300 strokes. Babe came to the 72nd hole needing a birdie four for 299. Six feet from the hole in three, she missed the putt.

"Oh well," she gasped to the gallery, "it would just have put me in a higher tax bracket." Like Babe, I am a golf professional. Unlike Babe, I never had to worry at the prospect of being vaulted into a higher tax bracket.

In 1953, in addition to competing, I was the LPGA publicity director and traveled 40,000 miles in my car into which I stuffed my clubs, my clothes, a typewriter, files, camera, tape recorder and promotional materials. I even tied the scoreboard to the top of the car.

I did advance publicity and helped increase the purses to a minimum $5,000 for 72 holes. By 1955, we had prize money of $150,000. We never dreamed of $1 million purses for the week, of 40 tournaments a year, or of becoming millionaires on the world's premier women's golf tour.

We loved our lifestyle and those pioneer days. I wrote then: "If I am ever tempted to complain about the strain of tournaments or woes of traveling, I remember the poor girls back home slaving over hot stoves. Then I know how lucky I am to own a golf swing that will keep me going on the LPGA circuit." I am proud to have helped lay the foundation for the LPGA's 50-year growth and onward.

Facing page: Pioneers Betty Hicks (left) and Patty Berg compete in 1942. **Above:** Betty Hicks.

THE LPGA STORY

In 1950, the year of the birth of the LPGA, Shirley Spork became a professional golfer in unusual circumstances. Spork recorded the event for the Ladies Professional Golf Association records:

BY LIZ KAHN

"While I was eating breakfast with Marilynn Smith and Babe and George Zaharias, prior to the first round of the Weathervane Women's Open in Chicago, Babe said to me 'Hey kid, why don't you turn pro? You are a top amateur from Michigan, we need more players like you on our ladies' tour.' I said: 'Babe, how do you turn pro?' She got up from the table, plonked her right hand down firmly on top of my head, and said 'Kid, you're a pro. Go tell them on the first tee you're playing as a pro.' I did and I was one of 11 women pros playing in that tournament."

Records indicate that the LPGA Certificate of Incorporation was signed in Wichita, Kan., during the U.S. Women's Open on September 30, 1950, by five young professionals: Patty Berg, Helen Dettweiler, Sally Sessions, Betty Jameson and Helen Hicks. Later on, Babe Zaharias, Alice and Marlene Bauer, Shirley Spork, Bettye Mims Danoff, Opal Hill, Louise Suggs and Marilynn Smith joined them as the 13 founding members of the LPGA.

The LPGA Tour can look back on these and other pioneers with pride. It was preceded by the Women's Professional Golf Association (WPGA), which was formed in 1944. The WPGA may not have been destined to become a major force, but it was an innovative organization comprised of women with special talents and drive. These pioneers subsequently made a significant impact on the evolution of women's professional golf and helped lay the foundation for the LPGA we know today.

Hope Seignious, a professional from North Carolina, was especially instrumental in the early effort. After meeting with golf professionals Betty Hicks and Helen Dettweiler, she persuaded her father to fund many of the tour's early activities, including the first women's golf magazine and the establishment of the first three National Women's Open Championships beginning in 1946.

In addition to Seignious, several other professionals such as Hicks, Dettweiler and Ellen Griffin emerged during this decade to help focus the spotlight on women's golf. Hicks, the first WPGA president, was a Renaissance woman who seemed to be ahead of her time. She was a pilot, a journalist, a gourmet cook, a cellist, painter, teacher and flight instructor. Only four years into her golf career, she won the 1941 National Amateur at The Country Club in Brookline, Mass., where the trophy was presented to her on the porch outside, as women could not enter the clubhouse.

Facing page: *Babe Zaharias was one of the best-known players of the early years. Her talent and outgoing personality always drew large crowds.*
Above: *The first emblem of the LPGA.*

WPGA Vice President Ellen Griffin, who died in 1985, founded national golf schools and trained hundreds of teachers through the years. She also wrote with Hicks, "The Golf Manual for Teachers," in 1949. Thus, they helped lay the seeds for the future founding of the LPGA's teaching division.

The late Helen Dettweiler, the WPGA's second president, seemed to do it all. She was the country's first woman radio baseball commentator in the 1930s, and during World War II she flew B-17s. She also was the first woman to design and build a nine-hole golf course, which was located in Palm Springs. She even gave golf lessons to President Dwight D. Eisenhower.

These were exceptional women. Their spirit, courage and inner strength motivated them through years of striving against barriers. They wanted to make their mark so that women in sport would be recognized and accepted.

The WPGA disbanded in 1949 and Hicks later conceded: "The first organization of women's professional golf was conceived in wrath, born into poverty and perished in a family squabble. The Women's Professional Golf Association was a bawling, scrawny child of early-day feminists, a beggar of a child pleading for tournaments and for amateurs to become professionals to play in them."

But the women were not ready to give up. A second effort was made to organize a women's professional golf tour. Fred Corcoran, of Wilson Sporting Goods, was named tournament manager of the tour in late 1949. And, he could not have wished for a more charismatic figure than Babe Zaharias to help him sell tournaments to sponsors. She was an essential ingredient to the successful launching of the tour. Even if she could infuriate at times with her flamboyance, her gift to the LPGA was in the giving of herself to a degree that was almost superhuman.

As the LPGA emerged in 1950, an extraordinary bond was formed between a small group of women whose common denominator was an abiding love of tournament golf. Naturally, there were gripes and petty conflicts, normal to any group of people traveling and living together for many weeks of the year, but humor was always near the surface.

Above: *"More than anything, Betty Jameson could make the ball dance, and it was beautiful" said Wiffi Smith. Jameson was known for her "sweet" swing.*

Left: *(L to R) Rawls, Berg, Suggs, and Zaharias were the "Big 4" of women's professional golf during the first decade of the LPGA.*

Below: *In the early years, the players enjoyed a very close bond because they had to organize all aspects of the tournaments if they wanted to compete. (L to R) Jean Bauer, Isabel Ogilvie, Jane Cothran Jamison, Kathryn Hemphill, Patty Berg, Helen Dettweiler, Marion MacDougall.*

Babe Zaharias was constantly promoting women's golf. She never tired of being the LPGA's front woman.

LPGA meetings could sometimes provide an arena for strong discussions, and on one occasion, an official stenographer who had been hired to take the minutes, suddenly threw down her notebook and resigned in hysterics. Bev Hanson said: "There were so many motions on the floor at the same time, I got seasick."

In the 1950s, women's golf had to fight for its very survival. Corcoran wrote in his memoirs: "The announcement that we had formed the Ladies Professional Golf Association touched off a national storm of indifference."

The competitors had not only to play, but to run the tournaments themselves. From setting up the golf courses to making the pairings to signing the checks, they persevered. In the first year, there were 14 LPGA events, worth nearly $50,000 in total prize money. At that time, Zaharias and Patty Berg were the prominent players. Their style and personalities helped bring out the fans and raise awareness of the tour. As it turned out, the inaugural event, the $3,500 Tampa Open, was won by amateur Polly Riley, who finished five shots ahead of Louise Suggs.

If Patty Berg wasn't on the golf course competing, odds were she was on the practice tee holding one of her very entertaining golf clinics.

To help gain further recognition and awareness for the women golfers, a World Golf Hall of Fame was established in 1950. A committee elected seven great names in women's golf from past eras as charter honorees. A year later the committee added Zaharias, Berg, Suggs and Betty Jameson. But, it was almost two decades before it found a visible home and was renamed the LPGA Hall of Fame. The first inductees were the LPGA members who had previoulsy been elected to the World Golf Hall of Fame.

When Corcoran left the LPGA in 1953, Zaharias and Hicks took up the reins, running and promoting the tournaments, followed by several interim directors. Zaharias' death from cancer in 1956 was a huge blow to the tour, but players such as Betsy Rawls, Berg, Suggs and Smith continued to help the tour grow. By 1959 the LPGA Tour had 26 events and played for $200,000 in total prize money.

It was in 1961 that a period of some stability began when Leonard Wirtz took over the administrative leadership of the organization. Wirtz, known as "The General," was a former assistant sales manager for MacGregor Golf. Dynamic and forceful, he systematically upgraded the tour, and it thrived under his direction for eight years. "Lenny gave us policies we live with today in our constitution and bylaws. He did a lot of good things," Kathy Whitworth said. "He fought for us."

THE LPGA STORY

"In the earlier days we played every week because we wanted to play. Even if we won, we weren't going to make a fortune. The pace wasn't as fast, the pressure wasn't as intense, but you played for the love of it." Kathy Whitworth

Just as Corcoran had Zaharias, Wirtz had Mickey Wright, who became one of the greatest professional golfers ever. "I was tougher on Mickey than anyone out there, since she was the star," Wirtz said. "Mickey and I sometimes used to go fishing together early in the morning. I told her to put her money in stocks and taught her how to do it. The stock market became her second passion. She was a woman driven by perfection, and eventually it drove her off the tour. I've never seen a woman play golf like Mickey."

During the 1970s, David Foster, CEO of the Colgate-Palmolive Company, helped take the women's tour to another level. He loved golf and cared deeply for the LPGA. His company put up enormous sums of money for several tournaments worldwide. Colgate also used LPGA players as spokespersons in its television advertising. This exposure helped give the LPGA more credibility within the business world.

Tour professional Joyce Kazmierski said: "David did it in royal style and all the players traveled first class. I remember returning from the Far East when Carol Mann had an eight-foot spear and 27 pieces of checked baggage. Colgate paid an excess baggage charge of $18,000."

Ray Volpe was the next dynamic force to affect the LPGA, arriving as its first commissioner in 1975. He lovingly and energetically created a golden era with Nancy Lopez as his star.

Lopez captured the imagination of the public and attracted television, which brought women's golf into millions of households. She made a startling impact not experienced since Babe Zaharias, whom she did not resemble at all. Lopez was not a superb athlete; she was the girl next door with shining eyes, a quick smile and glossy hair whose golf achievements and delightful personality bowled over the public and media, alike.

With Volpe, the electricity was tangible: "My job is to promote the well-being of 160 players," he said. "But I can capitalize on Nancy, because when she smiles there is not a smile like that in the whole world."

In addition, Volpe set up an LPGA board of directors that included members of the corporate world. It was the first time that the administration of the organization was taken out of the players' domain. This led to an era of financial expansion. In 1981 the LPGA reached a landmark in sport as Volpe introduced the organization's retirement program — the first deferred compensation plan for athletes in a non-team professional sport.

Expansion and a hiccup or two continued through the 1980s, but the greatest change came with the increasing international flavor of the LPGA Tour. Although the tour had a few overseas professionals joining its group in the '70s and '80s, in the decade leading up to the millennium it was more like an international invasion.

Facing page, top left: *Nancy Lopez took the tour by storm in 1978, capturing both the Rolex Rookie of the Year and Player of the Year honors;* **bottom left:** *Kathy Whitworth could always find a way to win, as evidenced by her record 88 career titles;* **right:** *With her picture-perfect swing and 82 career victories, Mickey Wright is heralded by many as the greatest woman golfer ever.*

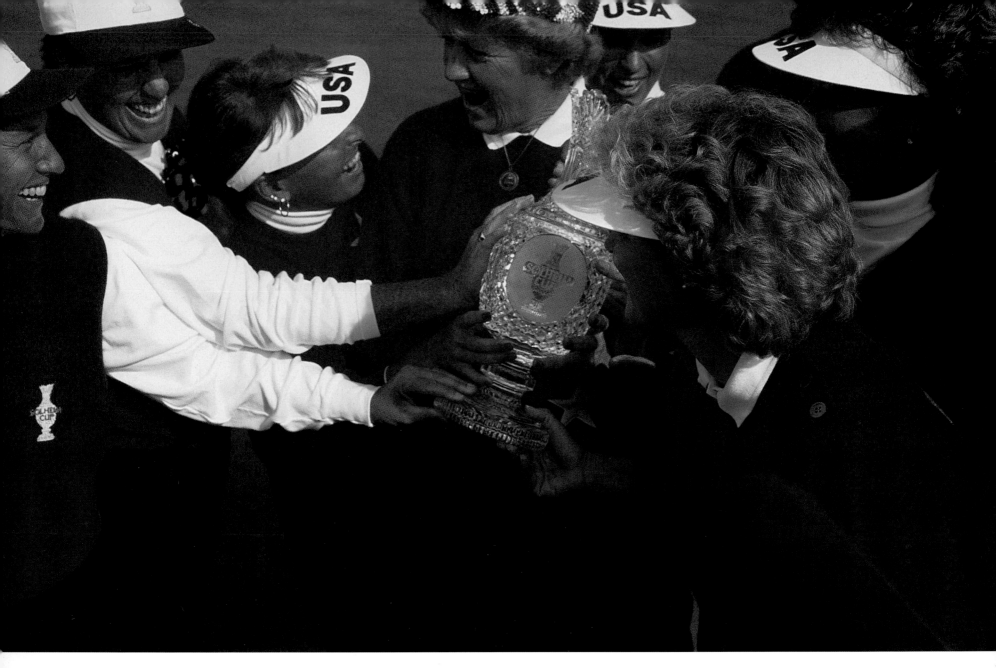

The winning U.S. Solheim Cup team in 1994 surrounds team captain JoAnne Carner. The growing number of European players competing on the LPGA Tour encouraged the establishment of The Solheim Cup in 1990.

In 1987, Laura Davies from England exploded onto the scene by winning the U.S. Women's Open in a rain-delayed, three-way playoff over JoAnne Carner and Ayako Okamoto. It was the year before Davies joined the tour, and the LPGA passed an amendment to its bylaws giving the Open champion exemption from LPGA Qualifying School. Davies was a breath of fresh air; she charmed the crowds with her shy but friendly personality. She gambled, loved shopping, never took golf lessons and she hit the ball farther than any woman golfer ever had. In 1979 Davies spearheaded a European influx to the LPGA Tour. Sweden's Liselotte Neumann won the 1988 U.S. Open and Annika Sorenstam dominated for four seasons from 1995, when she captured the U.S. Women's Open and successfully defended her title the following year. Australian Karrie Webb made her sensational impact with 15 victories in four seasons from 1996 through 1999. The LPGA needed this international influence and that's what it got. In fact, this influence encouraged the establishment of The Solheim Cup. It began in 1990 and pitted the LPGA's best against the top Europeans.

Top left: *Laura Davies' U.S. Women's Open victory in 1987 marked the beginning of an influx of Europeans onto the tour.* **Bottom left:** *Liselotte Neumann was the first Swedish player to win an LPGA major.* **Right:** *Hiromi Kobayashi of Japan qualified for the tour on her first attempt in 1990.*

"We have the quality, talent, and ability to justify a level of acceptance above what we've historically achieved."

Charles S. Mechem Jr., LPGA Commissioner (1990-1995)

Through its history, the LPGA has absorbed and been affected by a variety of factors, which have brought about change and progression. Feminism and Title IX in the 1970s had parts to play, as did the sex symbols through the decades. Betty Jameson and the Bauer sisters were the glamorous youngsters at its inception, while Laura Baugh and Jan Stephenson sailed with great aplomb through the 1970s and onward.

Although the tour has needed its stars and motivators, the supporting cast has been its essential ingredient. Each round of golf played, each lesson given or club sold is a reflection of the spirit of the LPGA women.

LPGA Hall of Famer Rawls, who would have been a physicist had she not turned to golf, said it best: "The tour has survived so well because of the character of the players. The biggest contributing factor is that over the years they remained so nice. They were never arrogant or too temperamental; they made themselves liked with something more than their golf. In the beginning, they realized they had to give something to the sponsors. They played golf with them and gave them their friendship. There was not a lot of money in those days, but the sponsors came back because they liked the women." This is a proud heritage to carry into the 21st century.

Sweden's Catrin Nilsmark was a member of the 1998 European Solheim Cup team and captured her first LPGA victory in 1999.

Babe Zaharias often impressed the crowds with her wonderful short game. Betsy Rawls said of Babe, "If it hadn't been for Babe, [the LPGA] probably wouldn't have survived. She gave the organization immediate credibility and brought people out to watch."

Marilynn Smith received congratulations from Mickey Wright after her winning putt at the Titleholders Championship. Smith won back-to-back Titleholders Championships in 1963 and 1964.

Left: *JoAnne Carner was known as "Big Mama" on the tour. Her humor and engaging personality endeared her to players and fans.* **Center:** *Jane Blalock won 27 tournaments in the 1970s, but never won a major championship.* **Right:** *Kathy Whitworth had such a talent for winning that she was named LPGA Player of the Year four consecutive times in the 1960s and was the first to cross $1 million in career earnings.*

Hollis Stacy's three U.S. Women's Open victories make her one of only five women to have won the championship three or more times.

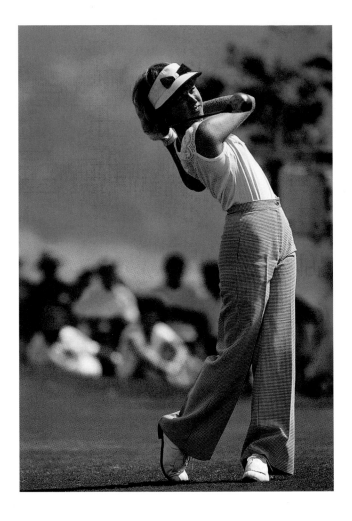

From long skirts to bell-bottoms to today's sleek contemporary look, fashion has always been as individual as the players themselves.

Top, left: *Laura Baugh;* **right:** *Sandra Haynie and Barbara Romack.*

Bottom, left: *Betsy Rawls, Louise Suggs, Marilynn Smith;* **right:** *JoAnne Carner.*

Top, left: *Michelle McGann;* **right:** *Grace Park.*
Bottom, left: *Sophie Gustafson;* **right:** *Jackie Gallagher-Smith.*

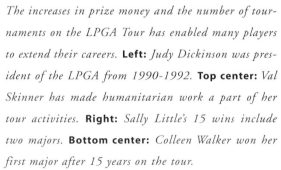

The increases in prize money and the number of tournaments on the LPGA Tour has enabled many players to extend their careers. **Left:** *Judy Dickinson was president of the LPGA from 1990-1992.* **Top center:** *Val Skinner has made humanitarian work a part of her tour activities.* **Right:** *Sally Little's 15 wins include two majors.* **Bottom center:** *Colleen Walker won her first major after 15 years on the tour.*

Nancy Scranton celebrated her 14th year (1999) on the tour with her best season ever, enjoying seven top-10 finishes. Then, she began the 2000 season with a third career victory at the Subaru Memorial of Naples in Florida.

Facing page: *Donna Andrews' six career victories include the 1994 Nabisco Dinah Shore.* **Above:** *Alison Nicholas defeated crowd favorite Nancy Lopez at the 1997 U.S. Women's Open, for her first major win on The LPGA Tour.*

Above: *In 1955, eight of the founders were joined by six other pioneers. (L to R) back row: L. Lobo, J. Pung, B. Dodd, B. Hicks, B. McKinnon, B. Zaharias, M. Bauer, A. Bauer, F. Crocker; front row: P. Berg, L. Suggs, B. Rawls, B. Jameson, M. Smith.*

Below: *The eight living founders assembled for an LPGA 50th Anniversary event. (L to R) back row: M. Smith, M. Hagge, A. Bauer, B. Jameson, L. Suggs; front row: B. Danoff, P. Berg, S. Spork.*

THE LPGA FOUNDERS

Thirteen women with one dream. That's how the founders of the LPGA could be described when they sat together in 1950 at Rolling Hills Country Club in Wichita, Kansas.

BY LISA D. MICKEY

Their dream was to charter a women's professional golf tour with regular tournament stops and respectable purses. And those original 13 were willing to lead the way in promoting their own tour from the start.

"We were dreamers and we were a small group, but everybody bonded together to make it go," said Marilynn Smith, one of the 13. "We came from all backgrounds and parts of the country, but each of us brought her own charisma and capability to the birth of the organization."

The LPGA's formation actually stemmed from an idea by Babe Didrikson Zaharias' agent Fred Corcoran, who wanted an association that would showcase his client's immense talent. Zaharias used Wilson Golf equipment, so fellow Wilson players Patty Berg, Helen Dettweiler and Opal S. Hill, signed up to play. Spalding players Betty Jameson and Smith, as well as MacGregor's Louise Suggs, also joined. The other players who signed the charter were sisters Alice Bauer and Marlene Bauer Hagge, Bettye Danoff, Helen Hicks, Sally Sessions and Shirley Spork.

Zaharias was "the Olympic name" who drew the crowds with her renowned athleticism and quick quips, but fans quickly learned there were other stars, including those who beat the tournament draw. Danoff, in fact, was the player who ended Zaharias' 17-game winning streak.

Galleries greatly appreciated Berg, the shotmaker, as well as the classic swing of Suggs. Unlike Berg and Zaharias, Suggs was the quiet type, but she contributed greatly behind the scenes. Smith was the outgoing ambassador of the tour, while the Bauer sisters and Jameson were the LPGA's early "glamour girls."

Some of the players, such as Danoff and Alice Bauer, eventually left golf to rear families. Spork, Hill and Dettweiler became teaching professionals. Sessions became a high school teacher, while Berg, Hagge, Jameson, Smith, Suggs and Zaharias made their respective marks as touring pros. The eight surviving founders continue to support the LPGA Tour. "It is a tribute to the founders that golf is now a lifetime career opportunity for women," said Smith. "And it was fun."

Above: *The Women's Titleholders Championship Trophy*

Top, left: *Helen Hicks was the first woman to sign a contract with a sporting goods company;* center: *Marlene Bauer Hagge;* right: *Bettye Danoff.* Center: *Alice Bauer* Bottom, left: *Opal Hill;* center: *Sally Sessions was one of the first officers of the LPGA;* right: *Shirley Spork was a pioneer of the LPGA Teaching Division.*

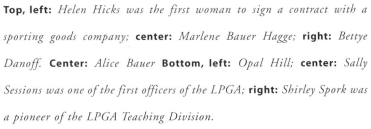

Top, left: *Patty Berg was the first president of the LPGA;* **center:** *Louise Suggs served as LPGA president three times;* **right:** *Helen Dettweiler.* **Center:** *Babe Zaharias won six of the 11 tournaments in the LPGA's inaugural year.* **Bottom, left:** *Betty Jameson created the Vare Trophy in 1952 to honor the player with the lowest season-scoring average;* **right:** *Marilynn Smith was instrumental in the development of the LPGA Teaching Division.*

LPGA Tour Hall of Fame

From a small beginning at the Augusta Country Club, the LPGA Tour Hall of Fame has now found its home in a grand resting place with the World Golf Hall of Fame at the World Golf Village in St. Augustine, Florida.

BY LIZ KAHN

It all started in 1950 when Fred Corcoran, the first LPGA tournament director, came up with an idea to recognize the achievements of the greatest women golfers of the past by establishing a Women's World Golf Hall of Fame.

Corcoran formed an action committee of six national journalists and met with them at the Augusta Country Club during the Masters Tournament. The committee elected great women golfers from former eras as charter honorees: Beatrix Hoyt, Alexa Stirling Fraser, Dorothy Campbell Hurd, Virginia Van Wie, Margaret Curtis, Glenna Collett Vare and British golfer Joyce Wethered (Lady Heathcott

Amory). A year later the committee met again and added Babe Zaharias, Patty Berg, Betty Jameson and Louise Suggs. Though there was no official criteria at that time, honorees were chosen for their outstanding achievements in golf.

It was nine years before Betsy Rawls became the next player elected to the Hall of Fame in 1960. She posted 10 victories in 1959 alone and was the leading money-winner with $26,744. At that time, Rawls had a total of 40 tournament victories, including three of her four U.S. Women's Open titles. She went on to win 53 events, including eight major championships in her career. "You just received a telegram to say you had been elected," Rawls recalled.

Facing page: *Nancy Lopez qualified for the LPGA Tour Hall of Fame in 1987 and that year was also named "Golfer of the Decade" by GOLF Magazine.* **Above:** *The World Golf Hall of Fame houses a vast collection of golf memorabilia, including collectibles from the LPGA and its members.*

Above: *Babe Zaharias won 10 major championships in her career.*

Right: *Of Betty Jameson's 13 career victories, she won four events in 1955 alone.*

Facing page, top: *Louise Suggs' 58 victories include setting the all-time record for margin of victory of 14 strokes, at the '49 U.S. Women's Open. This record still stands today;* **bottom:** *Patty Berg holds the LPGA record for the most major championship titles with 15.*

Members:

1951	Patty Berg, 60 career victories
	Betty Jameson, 13 career victories
	Louise Suggs, 58 career victories
	Babe Zaharias, 41 career victories
1960	Betsy Rawls, 55 career victories
1964	Mickey Wright, 82 career victories
1975	Kathy Whitworth, 88 career victories
1977	Sandra Haynie, 42 career victories
	Carol Mann, 38 career victories
1982	JoAnne Carner, 43 career victories
1987	Nancy Lopez, 48 career victories
1991	Pat Bradley, 31 career victories
1993	Patty Sheehan, 35 career victories
1995	Betsy King, 32 career victories
1999	Amy Alcott, 29 career victories
	Beth Daniel, 32 career victories
	Juli Inkster, 22 career victories
2000	Judy Rankin, 26 career victories
1994	Dinah Shore, Honorary member

Betsy Rawls tees off at the '57 U.S. Women's Open on her way to her third of four U.S. Open Titles.

"I thought I was going to be a winner and as I went along, winning became easier and easier," Rawls said. "It was something I expected to do. I always played well under pressure because it didn't bother me, which is why I won so many tournaments. I could perform under tense situations. My physical makeup allowed it to happen."

Mickey Wright entered the Hall in 1964 after she had 53 victories, including eight majors. Known for her perfect swing, she went on to win a total of 82 events in an amazing 26-year career. "I got winning and golf and myself very closely tied up," Wright said. "Golf was me and I was nothing without golf."

Mickey Wright won 13 tournaments in 1963 – an LPGA record that has never been matched.

Kathy Whitworth won the last of her 88 titles in 1985, setting a record which has never been surpassed by any other professional golfer in history, male or female.

Top left: *JoAnne Carner remains the last amateur to win an LPGA event, the '69 Burdine's Invitational.* **Bottom left:** *In 1968, Carol Mann claimed 10 titles and won the Vare Trophy with an average score of 72.04, a record that held until 1978.* **Right:** *Sandra Haynie recorded 39 victories from 1961-76 before arthritis began to hinder her participation on the tour.*

Two-time Rolex Player of the Year, Pat Bradley, was named captain of the 2000 U.S. Solheim Cup Team.

Three years later in 1967, the members of the LPGA established the LPGA Hall of Fame. It was different from the World Golf Hall of Fame in that it limited initiation into the Hall to LPGA members, and to enter it one had to meet specific performance criteria. The first inductees were LPGA Tour players already in the Women's World Golf Hall of Fame: Berg, Jameson, Suggs, Zaharias, Rawls and Wright. Over the decades Kathy Whitworth, Sandra Haynie, Carol Mann, JoAnne Carner, Nancy Lopez, Pat Bradley, Patty Sheehan and Betsy King fulfilled the criteria and joined this elite group. And, in 1994, Dinah Shore was named the first Honorary Member of the Hall of Fame. Shore, who is often referred to as "the first lady of women's golf," spent more than three decades promoting the LPGA Tour, and her legacy lives on through The Nabisco Championship, one of the LPGA's four major championships.

The tough requirements of the LPGA Hall of Fame made it one of the most difficult of all sports achievements. A player must have been an LPGA member for 10 consecutive years. She also must have won at least 30 official events, including two majors, or 35 events with one major title or have 40 wins with no majors. And until 1974, the player had to have been retired for two years before she could get into the prestigious Hall. Kathy Whitworth, who qualified in 1967 on all counts except retirement, had to wait until 1974 for that criterion to be dropped. She was then inducted in 1975. And, when Nancy Lopez qualified for entry in 1987 and Annika Sorenstam in 2000, they also had to wait to become members.

Above: *Betsy King, who did not win a tournament in her first seven years on tour, won 20 tournaments between 1984 and 1989. Entering 2000, she continued to be ranked number one in career earnings.* **Left:** *Patty Sheehan's six major championships include two U.S. Women's Open titles. Patty followed her Rolex Rookie of the Year award in 1981 with the Rolex Player of the Year award and the Vare Trophy in 1984.*

> *"Tremendous humility coupled with tremendous talent. That's what makes champions out of great players."* Debbie Massey

Following Lopez' induction, there was a four-and-a-half-year hiatus before Pat Bradley became the 12th member of the Hall of Fame in 1991. Patty Sheehan followed in 1993 and Betsy King in 1995. Discussions about revising the challenging requirements to make it a less exclusive group were held frequently through the years. Some thought that new entrants might dwindle to almost none as international players flooded the ranks and as the tour continued to grow.

But opinion was divided about changing the criteria. Fourteen phenomenal players had gotten in under the stringent requirements. "Not everyone was meant to be in the Hall of Fame," Mickey Wright commented. However, those in favor of opening the gates to a wider circle prevailed and the requirements were amended in 1999.

The new guidelines for entry into what is now called the LPGA Tour Hall of Fame are based on a point system. Entry requires a total of 27 points, with two points awarded for a major championship, one point for winning an LPGA event and one point each for winning the Player of the Year award or the Vare Trophy (awarded to the player with the lowest scoring average of the season). The entrant also must have been an active member for 10 years.

After the amendments were made, most of the earlier Hall of Fame members were supportive: "The committee that framed the new requirements is to be appreciated and applauded for its conscientious, thoughtful and contemporary plan," Hall of Famer Carol Mann said. "I voted for it without equivocation."

Despite qualifying for the Hall of Fame in February 1987, Nancy Lopez had to wait six months to fulfill the 10-year active member requirement.

Top left: *In 1990, Beth Daniel captured seven of her 32 victories and set a record, scoring nine consecutive rounds in the 60s.*

Top right: *In recognition of her contributions to the LPGA Tour, Dinah Shore was named as the first honorary member of the Hall of Fame in 1994.*

Bottom: *In 1991, Amy Alcott won the Nabisco Dinah Shore for the third time and her 29th career victory.*

Facing page: *Juli Inkster's fifth victory of 1999 at The Safeway LPGA Championship qualified her for entry into the Hall of Fame.*

"We all knew well that fragile thread of winning. We knew we could be going along, and if some little thing came up, if we strayed, it would make all the difference." Betty Jameson

In 1999, LPGA professionals Amy Alcott, Beth Daniel and Juli Inkster all qualified for entry. Alcott and Daniel, eligible as soon as the new criteria passed, marched right in. Alcott, with 29 victories including five majors, reminisced: "In 1982 I was at the World Championship of Women's Golf. I stood on the 18th green and JoAnne Carner made this beautiful putt that clinched her Hall of Fame arrival. As the light came through the trees, I thought: 'That is really where I want to be some day.' It gave me a carrot to grab at and a wonderful special moment to share with JoAnne. It has been a long road. But now this is really a crowning achievement in my life."

Daniel, who had 32 victories including one major, said: "I can say that looking at our careers, I honestly felt we were Hall-of-Famers and I am very honored to be part of it."

Inkster plowed her way into the Hall of Fame in 1999 with a phenomenal season. She had five victories, including the U.S. Women's Open and the McDonald's LPGA Championship. She was just edged out of Player of the Year and the Vare Trophy honors by sensational Australian Karrie Webb (who won six tournaments, taking her own total to 15 victories in just five years on tour). These wins carried Inkster to post 22 tournament victories, including five major titles, to ensure her place in the Hall.

The year 2000 began with Judy Rankin, a 26-time LPGA Tour champion, being voted into the Hall of Fame in the Veteran's category, which was created in February 1999. She became the 18th playing member.

When Inkster became a member of the Hall of Fame, she commented, "These are the ladies who have made the LPGA what it is today. I was fortunate to have played with Whitworth, Carner, Bradley, King, Lopez, Sheehan, Alcott and Daniel. I look up to and respect them a great deal because they have sacrificed a lot in their careers to make the LPGA what it is today. It is really hard for me to think of myself in that company." But there she is, where she belongs with the other greats of women's professional golf.

Brandie Burton, 1998 du Maurier Classic

Sandra Haynie, 1966 Buckeye Savings Invitational

Annika Sorenstam, 1996 U.S. Women's Open

Juli Inkster, 1999 McDonald's LPGA Championship

Betsy King with Dinah Shore, 1990 Nabisco Dinah Shore

Helen Alfredsson, 1993 Nabisco Dinah Shore

Se Ri Pak, 1999 PageNet Championship

Mickey Wright, 1961 U.S. Women's Open

Hiromi Kobayashi, 1998 Japan Classic

ON TOUR

When Patty Berg won her first professional tournament at the 1941 Western Open, the top prize was a $100 savings bond. That's in stark contrast to the $315,000 that Juli Inkster pocketed for winning the 1999 U.S. Women's Open.

BY LISA D. MICKEY

The numbers alone show just how much the times have changed. And that's a good thing for the LPGA, growing from 13 American pros in 1950 to 350 touring pros from 20 nations entering the new century. The tour's pioneers once played a nine-tournament season worth a total of $50,000 in prize money,

which seems paltry, compared to the modern era's $36.2 million season purses for 43 events. What's more, today's multinational tour makes stops in Canada, Australia, Great Britain, Europe and Japan as a part of its official schedule.

Berg's professional career hopscotched wherever she could find a game, "I remember when we had three or four tournaments and played for $500," said Berg, 82.

In the early years, an entire field would play a complete season for nearly the same amount that a modern-era player earns for sixth place in a $1.4 million event. For a record 88 tournament wins in 33 seasons, Kathy Whitworth pocketed $1.7 million in prize money. By contrast, Karrie Webb earned nearly $1.6 million in 25 weeks in 1999.

"Sometimes, it makes you want to lose your cookies," Louise Suggs, 76, once joked of the earning potential of today's touring pro.

Of course, the size of tournament purses is not the only gauge by which to measure the tour's growth. There have been numerous influences, including the role played by mass media. It was television that ultimately helped popularize women's professional golf, even though full tournament coverage was slow to arrive. If women's golf made it to television in the 1950s, it was only on newsreels. Then, in 1963, the U.S. Women's Open became the first televised women's golf event. It was 1982 before all four rounds of an LPGA event – the Nabisco Dinah Shore – were televised nationally. By 1990, 15 events were on television, improving to nearly 35 LPGA tournament broadcasts by the end of the century.

The tour's stars also have helped broaden global interest in the LPGA. Due to top international players, both past and present, such as Jan Stephenson and Webb of Australia, England's Laura Davies, Annika Sorenstam of Sweden, Ayako Okamoto and Hiromi Kobayashi of Japan, Se Ri Pak of South Korea and Canadians Sandra Post and Lorie Kane, tournaments are now telecast to more than 140 countries.

The growth has also benefited the communities hosting LPGA events, and national nonprofit organizations such as the Ronald McDonald House Charities have gained tremendously from the charitable activities associated with the LPGA Tour. The LPGA has helped raise more than $102 million for charity since 1981. The Susan G. Komen Breast Cancer Foundation is the tour's official national charity.

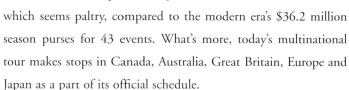

Above: *Nancy Scranton walks to victory at the 2000 Subaru Memorial of Naples after winning her first career playoff.*

Above: *Known as "Little Ben Hogan," Louise Suggs always drew large galleries.* **Facing page, top:** *Fans were awed by Mickey Wright's talent. She dominated the 1960s when she won 68 of her 82 career victories;* **bottom:** *Rosie Jones has always been a crowd favorite.*

The LPGA's major championships have also changed over the years. The Western Open was contested as a major from 1937 to 1967, while the Titleholders (dubbed the "women's Masters" because it was located in Augusta, Ga., and the invitees were the season's title holders) was held from 1937 to 1966 and again in 1972. Both enjoyed lengthy tenures alongside the U.S. Women's Open and the LPGA Championship (now called the McDonald's LPGA Championship).

Another change in recent years has been expansion of the LPGA's schedule, with events skipping across the Atlantic for the Weetabix British Women's Open, as well as to Canada, Australia, Japan and Korea. The European LPGA also has improved its schedule and purse, attracting more American-based LPGA players to come abroad to compete in Scotland, France and Sweden.

Stateside, midsize cities have remained the lifeblood of the LPGA's regular tour schedule. Those tour stops have typically drawn crowds for the LPGA because of the avid community support, often evidenced by the large number of tournament volunteers. Golf fans in those towns frequently decorate storefront windows and get the entire community involved. Often "the biggest game in town" is a welcome event for both the players and fans because small-town enthusiasm carries big-time appeal for top stars.

The 18th at Mission Hills Country Club is one of the most challenging finishing holes on the LPGA Tour.

Even as tournaments have changed over the years, four events stand out every season. They are distinguished by the prize purses offered, by the venues played and by the larger galleries they attract. They are the LPGA's major championships: The Nabisco Championship (formerly the Nabisco Dinah Shore), the U.S. Women's Open, the McDonald's LPGA Championship and the du Maurier Classic, four events worth more than $5.3 million by the end of the 1990s. In addition, The Solheim Cup, the biennial team matches between the top 12 players of both the United States and Europe, provides another special event and even more added excitement.

THE NABISCO CHAMPIONSHIP

The first major of the year is played at Mission Hills Country Club in Rancho Mirage, Calif., each March. The Nabisco Championship, affectionately called "The Dinah" by players and fans, is set in the Palm Desert oasis and is surrounded by the snowcapped San Jacinto Mountains. It's among the most picturesque sites visited by the LPGA, and the Dinah Shore Tournament Course is one of the finest tests that the women golfers face all year. Certainly, its water-bordered 18th is one of the game's most recognizable finishing holes and has historically featured a ceremonial swim by the champion. Some have galloped in, some have cautiously waded in, some have held their noses and plunged and some have dragged along the tournament's late namesake. Amy Alcott started that tra-

dition in 1991, after shooting 15 under par for the third of her three wins there. Since that time, fans have cheered for the winner to earn both her trophy and traditional white terry-cloth bathrobe.

"It's a special atmosphere with Hollywood ambiance and a lot of history," said Juli Inkster, a two-time champion who has avoided taking the water plunge both times. "There are some great finishing holes on that course and walking up the 18th fairway with everybody around the green is really something."

Dinah Shore was one of the first widely recognized celebrity entertainers to take an active interest in the LPGA. She teamed with Colgate for the event from 1972 to 1981, and invited her Hollywood pals to join the tournament's star-studded pro-am. Nabisco later took over sponsorship of the limited-field tournament that became a major championship in 1983.

Left: *In 1999, Dottie Pepper won her second Nabisco Dinah Shore Championship with a tournament record 19-under-par total.*
Above: *In 1996, Patty Sheehan took the traditional victory swim with her trophy.*

MCDONALD'S LPGA CHAMPIONSHIP

The LPGA Championship, now played in late June at DuPont Country Club in Wilmington, Del. — the tour's only regular East Coast stop for a major — has been contested since 1955, with Mazda serving as the title sponsor from 1987 to 1993, and McDonald's from 1994 to the present. It is the second-longest running tournament in LPGA history behind the U.S. Women's Open, and its list of past winners reads like a who's-who of women's golf, including former two-time champion and Hall-of-Fame member Betsy Rawls, who now serves as the event's executive

director. DuPont also was the site of Korean Se Ri Pak's first LPGA win in 1998 and Juli Inkster's second-in-a-season major in 1999 on her way to qualifying for the Hall of Fame.

This popular event typically attracts large galleries from the Washington, D.C., Baltimore, Philadelphia and New Jersey region. And its 2,500 community-based volunteers have made the tournament one of the best-run events on the tour. In addition to having up-close views of the top LPGA players all week, volunteers are motivated by the tournament's emphasis on support for children's charities. In 19 years, the event has raised $31.5 million to benefit Ronald McDonald House Charities in 23 countries. The tournament's role as a fund-raiser has made it one of the top contributors to charity among all sporting events.

Left: *In 1992, Betsy King won her fifth major at the Mazda LPGA Championship.* **Above:** *Ronald McDonald and friend celebrate the tournament's focus on charity.* **Facing page, top left:** *In 1997, Chris Johnson won her first major at the McDonald's LPGA Championship;* **top right:** *Kelli Kuehne cautiously studies the challenging course;* **bottom:** *"Hat Lady" Michelle McGann remains one of the most popular and recognizable players on the tour.*

U.S. WOMEN'S OPEN

When a golf course is long, tough and demanding, players frequently call it an "Open-style course." Translated, that means it bears a resemblance to the challenging venues selected by the United States Golf Association for the U.S. Women's Open, which moves to different courses and calendar dates during the summer months of each year.

The Women's Open, first won by Patty Berg in 1946, traditionally features some of the season's most difficult course setups, while also rewarding players with the year's highest purse. Winning the Open puts players in a special category. "It's the finest individual title I've ever won," said Laura Davies, who made her first American win the 1987 U.S. Open in a grueling 18-hole playoff against JoAnne Carner and Ayako Okamoto. "I'd trade in several victories for one Open," added Annika Sorenstam, who owns two Open titles. "To win a tournament like that is what you practice for. It gave me confidence and credibility."

There have been some spectacular finishes over the years at the Open, including eight 18-hole playoffs, one victory by an amateur (Catherine LaCoste) and six back-to-back wins by Mickey Wright (1958-59), Donna Caponi (1969-70), Susie Berning (1972-73), Hollis Stacy (1977-78), Betsy King (1989-90) and Annika Sorenstam (1995-96). One of the most compelling dramas in all of sports came in 1998 when Pak, a rookie, and amateur Jenny Chuasiriporn, a Duke University student, went into a playoff at the grueling, windy and long Blackwolf Run Golf Club in Kohler, Wis. The pair of 20-year-olds played 20 extra holes until Pak finally drained a long putt to end the marathon. The epic 92-hole tournament became the longest in women's professional golf history. And perhaps, the most memorable. A new generation was making its presence felt.

Above: *Lorie Kane is welcomed by record crowds at the Old Waverly Golf Club in Mississippi during the state's first Women's Open in 1999.*

Facing page, left: *At the 1998 Open, Jenny Chuasiriporn sank a 30-foot putt on the 18th that resulted in an epic 92-hole tournament that included a 20-hole playoff;* **right:** *Veterans (L to R) Jane Geddes, Meg Mallon and Nancy Lopez signaled their surrender to the difficult 1998 Blackwolf Run course.*

Left: *Karrie Webb won her first major title at the 1999 du Maurier.* **Center:** *Brandie Burton won her second du Maurier crown in 1998.* **Right:** *After barely making the cut,*
Nancy Scranton went on to win the 1991 du Maurier for her first win as an LPGA pro.

du MAURIER CLASSIC

The fourth and final major moves north of the border into Canada for the du Maurier Classic, which, like the Open, rotates to a different course each year and travels to a variety of regions throughout Canada. A major since 1979, the du Maurier is the LPGA's only stop in Canada and is a source of great pride for Canadian pros.

"It showcases our country and every Canadian wants to be in the field," said Lorie Kane, a native of Prince Edward Island. "The fans cheer like they're at a hockey game and I can tell you walking onto the first tee is nerve-racking for any Canadian."

Jocelyne Bourassa, now the tournament's executive director, won the inaugural title in 1973 in the event's forerunner, called La Canadienne. Heading into the new century, Bourassa remained the only Canadian to win the event – an accomplishment that may stand for the life of the tournament.

In recent years, the du Maurier has been the event where many players have earned their first tournament win. Cathy Johnston-Forbes, Nancy Scranton, Sherri Steinhauer, Tammie Green and Jenny Lidback all made their inaugural trip to the winner's circle on Canadian soil. At the 1999 tournament, Karrie Webb earned her first major championship of an already spectacular career in Alberta, Canada, with her mother, visiting from Australia, trailing along in her gallery. Webb birdied four of her last five holes to trim a three-shot deficit and win in dramatic come-from-behind fashion.

Right: *Canadians consider the du Maurier their women's national open. "It's like a hockey game out there," said Canadian Lorie Kane.*

Playing for your country is a pressure-packed experience, alleviated only by the camaraderie of the team format.

Top left: *Patty Sheehan is a four-time Cup participant.*

Top right: *Veteran team members, Dottie Pepper and Brandie Burton.*

Bottom left: *'96 team members (L to R) Pepper, Jones, Daniel, McGann.*

Bottom right: *The players' first battle begins on the practice range.*

Top left: *The European team's stalwart Laura Davies.*

Top right: *Catrin Nilsmark (left) and Annika Sorenstam.*

Bottom left: *Fans show their colors for their team.*

Bottom right: *Marie-Laure de Lorenzi (left) and Helen Alfredsson.*

Sometimes dreams live and die with a single shot. **Top, left:** *A tree becomes an obstacle for Joan Pitcock;* **right:** *Karrie Webb battles the elements.* **Bottom, left:** *Kris Tschetter;* **right:** *Shelley Hamlin.* **Preceding page:** *Meg Mallon.*

Golf is a game of imperfections, which makes it a constant challenge. **Above:** *Jenny Lidback met the challenge in 1995, winning her first title at the du Maurier Classic.*

ON TOUR **73**

To participate in tournament golf is to compete at the highest level on some of the world's best courses, to constantly face the unpredictable, to experience regional charms and to watch efforts rise and fall with a handful of numbers. Each tournament presents a unique challenge and visual experience, both on and off the course. In describing a pro's life, Pat Bradley said, "Wednesday is our only work day. Thursday through Sunday are our glory days."

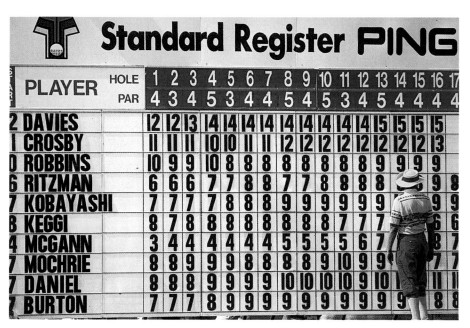

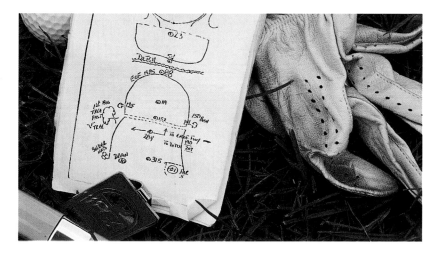

A PRO'S LIFE

There she was, the LPGA's Hat Lady, sitting in Chicago's O'Hare Airport terminal with her carry-on luggage, writing thank-you notes in calligraphy. Michelle McGann was about as far away from the glamorous spotlight of LPGA Tour life as she could be. She was dragging around her life in a bag on wheels and waiting for her ride in the sky to the next tour stop.

Surrounding her were several other players also en route to the next tournament. One shuffled through a pile of photographs of McGann's redecorated house in Florida. One thumbed through a handful of travel itineraries, while others rummaged through a bag of McDonald's breakfast food. It was an ordinary setting for an extraordinary nomadic lifestyle.

Ask any LPGA touring pro what she wants on the golf course and the answer is easy: a win or a top-10 finish. Then, ask a player who spends 26 to 35 weeks of the year on the road what she wants most of all, and the answer once again comes quickly: as "normal" a life as possible when one's home most often resembles a hotel room and the car is a rental.

In that regard, little has changed in 50 years, even though the mode of transportation and the number of players traveling to the next stop has. In the early days, air travel wasn't always an option. Betty Hicks and Peggy Kirk Bell both had pilot's licenses and sometimes flew their own planes, but they were the exceptions. Most players found their way to events by the highway in a convoy, resembling a migratory sorority.

Players often drove together or followed each other in caravans to cross-country destinations. Some players used a system of handmade signs that they held up in their car windows to indicate a need to stop for food, gas or stretch breaks. This is in vast contrast to the nearly 150 players who show up individually each week at modern events.

Most LPGA players today travel to the tournaments via commercial airlines and stay in hotels. Many players find that they achieve a sense of "normalcy" by staying in private housing during tournament week. For players just starting out, it is a smart way to save money on hotel costs. But even some high-profile players, such as Juli Inkster, have returned to the same private homes for years because their original hosts became close friends and the week's tournament is a good excuse for an annual reunion.

At the 1999 McDonald's LPGA Championship, Inkster seemed to thrive in the chaos of family, friends and tournament activities, and she ended up winning her second straight major of the year. Inkster's entourage consisted of her husband, a nanny, two daughters and one of her daughter's young pals. Her hosts, who have become good friends over the years, had five children of their own.

"It's wild," she said in the media interview room one day. "We had kids out the wing-wong last night. They were everywhere, but you know, I seem to play better when it's hectic like that."

That week, Inkster celebrated her 39th birthday with a cake at her host family's home and watched Women's World Cup soccer on television. She also took her kids to the pool, made sure the tooth fairy found her youngest daughter's pillow when she lost her first tooth and even cooked a French toast breakfast for 11 the morning of the final round. No wonder Inkster was at a loss for words later that sunny Sunday as the tournament's winner and could only warble, "Winner, winner, chicken dinner" when she was handed a microphone and a trophy.

Top: *In the 1950s, players traveled in closely-knit groups. They often gathered for sing-alongs during the evenings.* **Bottom:** *Today, players no longer travel in caravans, but they still enjoy getting together for activities, such as this fishing trip during their week at the LPGA Corning Classic.*

"Golfers aren't thought of as athletes. But to compete, you have to be an athlete. The stress and the pressures, the strain of holding your emotions in check through four days, the walking, the wind... It takes deep stamina to get you through to the end." *Kathy Whitworth*

Having a so-called "normal" life on tour is as difficult as it is unique. It is a balancing act that requires careful planning and organization. Nancy Lopez, for example, spends evenings in her hotel room talking to her daughters and husband on the telephone or tying up business matters for her company, Nancy Lopez Golf, a manufacturer of women's clubs. She pays bills and makes travel arrangements in the evenings so her mind is free to play golf the next day.

Karrie Webb often has dinner with her agent, who arranges business deals for the talented young Australian and helps her to adjust her schedule. Lorie Kane says she plans for road trips five weeks ahead of schedule and works to "develop a system" at each tournament site, carefully structuring time for practice, pro-am activities and personal needs so she has more time to spend with fans, sponsors and media.

"It's part of my responsibility of being a professional athlete to always be in control of what I do, both inside and outside the ropes," said Kane, who worked with contacts she had made playing weekly pro-am events to secure her own initial endorsements. Corporate endorsements help many young players financially in their early years on tour. For example, South Korean Se Ri Pak came to the LPGA with one large corporate contract with Samsung. She went on to win two major championships in her stellar rookie year in 1998.

While corporate sponsorships help alleviate some of the pressure to perform immediately, there is still the challenge of experiencing a "normal" life while traveling weeks on end. One of the ways many players make themselves feel at home on the road is to take along their dogs.

Left: *Emilee Klein had two wins and 19 top-10 finishes during her first four years on tour.* **Above:** *Laura Davies brings along a whimsical pup as her club headcover.* **Facing page:** *Karrie Webb made a seamless transition to the LPGA Tour with four wins in her rookie season.*

There are about 15 players who travel with dogs on a regular basis. It's not unusual to see a parade of morning dog walkers, including Liselotte Neumann with Pee Wee, the miniature Maltese who once took a victory lap around the 18th green at Moon Valley Country Club when Neumann won the 1998 Standard Register PING, and Emilee Klein with Callie. Callie, a Shih Tzu, has learned to open luggage zippers and decorate the hotel room with scattered clothes while Klein is at the course.

Wiffi Smith traveled with her piano and her dog while touring.

There are also plenty of activities that allow the pros to escape their day-job personae. As avid sports fans, many players will drive miles to unwind and watch professional baseball, ice hockey and WNBA games. Concerts also are popular getaways, as are the blackjack and craps tables during the PageNet Championship in Las Vegas and the ShopRite Classic near Atlantic City, N.J. The European players and caddies are a particularly close bunch and it's not uncommon for them to start up a soccer or cricket match in a vacant field near a tournament site. You can even find Laura Davies serving up a tennis ball about as hard as she hits her driver.

As fitness is a top priority for the pros, the LPGA offers a traveling fitness van to its members. The HealthSouth Sports Medicine Trailer has become an integral part of many players' training or physical rehabilitation from injuries. The tour also has a sizable group of players who participate in religious studies, as well as those who volunteer to work with the youngsters in the LPGA Tour's junior golf clinic program or to promote charitable activities.

Perhaps the tour program that has had the greatest impact on players has been the Smucker's LPGA Child Development Program. It is professional sport's only traveling child development facility, and it allows playing moms to focus on their jobs with greater ease. Players drop their children off at the center before they go to the course, then pick them up when the day is done. The program offers a structured day of play, education, meals and naps for the children and gives the professionals an option to completely leaving the tour to raise a family. As many as 50 children, ranging from four months to 11 years, participate in any given week.

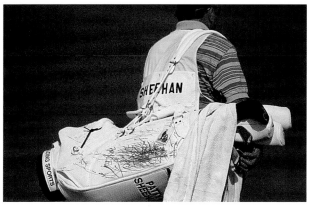

Top left: *Laura Baugh has raised seven children while competing on tour.*
Top right: *LPGA Child Development Center Director Tony Verive.*
Bottom left: *Patty Sheehan's bag carries featured "artwork" by her daughter.*
Bottom right: *Pepper, Sheehan, Davies, Lopez and many other tour members make charitable activities a regular part of their schedules.*

"Having a child development program was huge in my decision to have a child," said player Denise Killeen, whose husband John Killeen caddies for Meg Mallon. "Otherwise, you'd put off having a family. It allows the kids to have some normalcy. They see the same kids, the same toys, the same furniture and everything is familiar to them, week after week, because the tour moves it all from tournament to tournament. My son, Drew, enjoys it enough that he doesn't want to leave."

Above: *Tammie Green has recorded seven tour victories, including one major.* **Facing page, left:** *Players perform a few "housekeeping" tasks on the green;* **center:** *Cathy Johnston-Forbes, winner of the 1990 du Maurier, consults with caddie/husband Foster;* **right:** *Donna Andrews celebrates her win at the 1994 PING/Welch's Championship.*

"You may lose your health, you may lose your wealth, but if you lose your courage, you have lost everything. Courage is the prime requisite of a champion, golfer or otherwise." Opal Hill

The LPGA has addressed the needs of its members in many ways, allowing this microcosm of humanity to function like a traveling town. From fitness and club-repair vans, to the child development center, chaplains, on-site guest speakers and competitive earning opportunities within the tournament for veteran players, the tour has found more ways to make travel much easier for players and their families.

And, while LPGA players may never truly experience a so-called "normal" life on the tour, they are taking every opportunity to make it feel that way.

The thrill of walking up the 18th fairway on Sunday to the roar of an appreciative gallery can rarely be matched in most other day-to-day occurrences. Still, the memories linger and the organizational and personal contact skills that enabled these free agents to survive such a nomadic life will remain forever intact. After all, competition is survival of the fittest. In professional golf, the fit may be those who possess supportive family and friends, resilient temperaments, reliable corporate sponsorships, comfortable mattresses for a good night's sleep and a solid putting stroke. Every single element adds up in the career of a touring pro.

Wright is simply 'Awesome, awesome, awesome'

Fame comes easily
for vibrant Alcott

Cancer Fatal
at Babe

ON TOUR

Today, the demands of the media on tour professionals such as Se Ri Pak **(above)***, are in contrast to the struggle for public attention faced by players in the early years.*

ON TOUR

Caddies are that extra set of eyes, a second opinion for a crucial choice, or simply that special partner with whom to celebrate success.

Facing page: *Pat Hurst, winner of the 1998 Nabisco Dinah Shore, approaches the green during the 1998 Solheim Cup matches.*

Top, left: *Si Re Pak's caddie, Jeff "Tree" Cable, has helped to guide her since her rookie year in 1998;* **right:** *Canadian Dawn Coe-Jones has three career victories since joining the tour in 1984.* **Bottom:** *Kristi Albers celebrates her win at the 1993 Sprint Classic.*

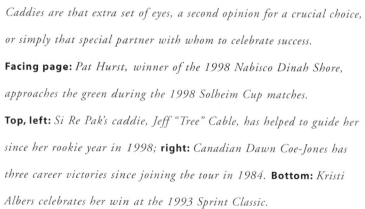

Above: *Dottie Pepper and PGA player Jeff Sluman team up in the mixed-team JCPenney Classic. Such events give players from the men's and women's tours a chance to compete together.* **Facing page:** *Kris Tschetter has been a frequent top-10 finisher since winning the 1992 Northgate Computer Classic.*

FIVE DECADES OF CHAMPIONS

Since the beginning of the LPGA Tour in 1950, each decade has witnessed a number of outstanding players and personalities. Whether cruising the country in caravans, championing women's rights or blending career and family, their lives have always been public.

BY MELANIE HAUSER

These women found themselves playing their way around the world – and into our lives through newspapers, magazines and television. We remember the smiles, the belly flops into the water, the hairstyles and their spirit. We celebrate the way they play the game and the way they not only reflect the times in which they played, but the way they often helped define those decades.

THE FIFTIES

They toured the country in big convertibles with the tops down and their hair blowing in the breeze. They wore fabulous pleated slacks and twinsets, tailored skirts and heathered tweeds. They were Katharine Hepburn, Bette Davis and Lauren Bacall rolled into one — a group of tough but tender women whose love for the game transcended any traditional role society thought they should play.

These were the pioneers: Women who had let the fabulous and often outrageous Babe Didrikson Zaharias lead them into the 50's, by marching into an office and promising a businessman he wouldn't regret sponsoring a golf tournament for women. In

fact, he'd make money doing it. Now, as the world was coming out of the war years, Babe and the women traveling with her saw a chance to take their loosely structured group and form an organization — the LPGA.

Babe, of course, took the spotlight. She always did. An athlete who was Title IX before it was drafted, she was an entertainer who never passed up the chance to promote herself — and the game. Even as she struggled with the cancer that ultimately took her life, Babe was the one everyone wanted to see. But she was hardly the only personality to define the decade.

Exuberant Patty Berg just about invented golf clinics and she taught manners, too. A sprite of a woman, she was a second lieutenant in the Marines during World War II, but she also directed the players to put their best ladylike foot forward — OK, Babe was the exception — by urging them to dress (gloves included) for airplane travel and dinner.

Then there was Betty Jameson, the game's first glamour girl. Jameson had a fragility to her and an artist's eye, but she was a tremendous amateur player whose short career as a pro was highlighted with a win at the 1947 U.S. Women's Open.

Facing page: *Marilynn Smith won 21 tournaments, including two majors during her years on the tour.* **Above:** *Juli Inkster was on fire in 1999, winning five titles, including two majors.*

Above: *Betty Jameson, the LPGA's first glamour girl, always wore her pearls to compete.* **Bottom, left:** *Louise Suggs, a quiet, intense player, was nicknamed "Miss Sluggs" by Bob Hope;* **right:** *Patty Berg, known as "the perky one" holds 60 career titles.*

Babe Zaharias wowed the galleries with her powerful swing. She was a "bigger-than-life, swaggering, confident hero," said Mickey Wright.

Louise Suggs was the Ben Hogan of the group. In fact, she even teamed with him in a "pro-lady" event, as they were called at that time. A quiet, precise player, "Miss Sluggs," as Bob Hope called her, received the winner's paycheck at the first official LPGA event because the player who finished first — Polly Riley — was an amateur. Suggs wasn't humorless, but she did draw the line at some of Babe's antics, something not many players of that day did.

The supporting cast was filled with colorful characters like: Peggy Kirk Bell, a licensed pilot who flew her Cessna 170 to tournaments and became one of the most respected teachers and businesswomen in the game; the fashionable and outgoing founder Marilynn Smith, who introduced pro-ams and press cocktail parties to the women's game; the Bauers, Marlene and Alice, the LPGA's first sister duo; and Wiffi Smith, whose career ended when she was 24 because of a hand injury.

FIVE DECADES OF CHAMPIONS

THE SIXTIES

The '60s was a decade of change in America. Civil rights and women's rights became not just issues, but causes. The British invaded the culture — in music and fashion. Camelot and its starched-collar, black-and-white images gave way to turbulent Technicolor that crept into every phase of life.

And, the LPGA Tour was no exception. What started as a decade of unflappable beehive hair — Kathy Whitworth's comes to mind — and fabulous golf from Mickey Wright and the cerebral Betsy Rawls, ended with Carol Mann's mod short hair and bright-colors look and Whitworth beginning to break almost every record in the book.

Whitworth debuted in 1959 at the Titleholders and when this lanky woman from a spot where Texas and New Mexico meet showed up on the practice range carrying a plaid bag, Wright couldn't help but blurt out, "What are you doing here?" Whitworth wasn't sure either, especially after finishing dead last. But it wasn't long until she started winning and spicing up the tour with her "fixin' tos" and "I reckons."

The careers of Whitworth, Rawls and Wright were intertwined like no others before or after. The three women were so different, yet so talented. Rawls was warm and intellectual. A Phi Beta Kappa in physics, she picked up the game at 17 and gave famed teacher Harvey Penick a lesson one day, explaining that instead of throwing a lot of thoughts at her, he might want to concentrate on one or two at a time. If a Phi Beta Kappa couldn't learn more than two things at a time, Penick reasoned, what chance did the rest of us have?

Rawls, a rookie in 1951, chose golf over a career in physics because, well, golf was more fun. Nine years later, she had won three of her four U.S. Women's Open titles. After retiring from the game in 1975, she became one of the most outstanding tournament directors in the country.

Above: *Betsy Rawls won 10 of her 55 career titles and the Vare Trophy in 1959.*
Facing page: *Marlene Hagge remains the youngest player to have won an LPGA event at 18 years and 14 days.*

Above: *Mickey Wright, "the soft-spoken legend," and Kathy Whitworth, (**facing page**) "the lanky Texan with the hair," dominated the tour in the 1960s, and in the process created a lifelong friendship.*

> *"Of all the players I've watched, men or women, nobody could swing a club as well as Mickey Wright."* Kathy Whitworth

Wright was the tour's soft-spoken darling. And the one to beat. Her command of the game was so impressive every shot captured attention — and gave the LPGA the boost it had needed since Babe's death in 1956. Together, Wright and Rawls captured eight of the 13 U.S. Women's Opens between 1951 and 1963, and their style won over fans and drew the crowds.

Whitworth may have started slowly, but she finished her career as the winningest player in the game, with a record 88 LPGA titles. She always had a fabulous short game, but she had to learn to control her swing and stand taller over the ball. That done, she was tough to stop.

Althea Gibson, the tennis star, traded her racquet for clubs and became the first black woman to play on the LPGA Tour. Renée Powell followed and both felt the sting of racial discrimination — especially in the South — but they didn't let it deter them from their careers. They played on in hopes of forcing the changes that finally came. And we're not talking about turning from caravanning across the country in cars to traveling by airplane.

Toward the close of the '60s, Mann, an imposing 6-foot-3 woman, stepped up her game and her profile. No longer content to simply play the game and watch women judged for their figures or sex appeal, Mann became an advocate for women's rights. She helped usher in the '70s by joining forces with those who eventually pushed for Title IX, which requires equal athletic opportunities for women and men in collegiate sports, and the creation of the Women's Sports Foundation.

Top left: *Althea Gibson, the first black woman to join the LPGA Tour, teamed with Jackie Robinson at the 1962 North/South Golf Tournament.*

Bottom Left: *A hole-in-one is every player's dream. Laura Baugh points out her single career hole-in-one at the 1972 Suzuki Golf Internationale.*

Right: *Sandra Palmer's powerful swing belied her small stature of 5'1".*
She recorded 19 career wins and was the Rolex Player of the Year in 1975.

THE SEVENTIES

It didn't take long for the players of the '70s to become leaders in the women's movement. Mann started it off and Jane Blalock added her voice. Judy Rankin became the first player to balance a top-10 career with a family, while Sandra Haynie proved women could keep winning into their 40s. Mann pushed hard for the tour's first commissioner, Ray Volpe. JoAnne Carner made the transition from amateur to pro; from The Great Gundy to Big Momma. Title IX opened the way for college scholarships, and LPGA players continued to push for change within what had been a static LPGA administrative system.

The results of their efforts were as disparate as the myriad of personalities involved.

While Laura Baugh and Jan Stephenson were being marketed as glamour poster girls, players like Rankin were deter-mined to let their talent speak for itself. In 1973, Rankin set a record that still stands with 25 top-10 finishes in a single season. She backed that up with outstanding years in 1976 and 1977 when she was the leading money-winner, Player of the Year and Vare Trophy winner both seasons — all while serving as the LPGA president. And raising a son.

Rankin was a tiny 5-foot-3, but she packed one heck of a punch. Soft-spoken but direct, she became the first player to pass the $100,000 mark in a season (1976) and became one of the most respected players on the tour. In addition to her stint as LPGA president, Rankin, who retired from the game because of back problems, became the first woman hired by a television network to work both men's and women's events. In the '90s, she captained two winning Solheim Cup teams.

A former president of the LPGA, Carol Mann is a national leader in the promotion of girls' and women's opportunities in sports.

50 STARS FROM 50 YEARS...

Ellen Griffin

Carol Mann

Kathy Whitworth

Clifford Ann Creed

Marilynn Smith

Hollis Stacy

Susie M Berning

Ruth Jessen

Jan Stephenson

Betsy Rawls

Sheila Englehorn

Louise Suggs

*"The press came out with the second-year jinx stories. I was really
determined to show them that I wasn't a flash in the pan.
I knew that I was winning because I was good enough to win.
It wasn't an accident."* Nancy Lopez

Outgoing Patty Sheehan was the other end of the spectrum. Another lone daughter in a family of competitive boys — and an Olympic ski coach for a dad — Sheehan was tough as nails, but fun to watch. She never led the money list, but in 1983, she was chosen to be the Rolex Player of the Year. She was always there pushing — herself and everyone else to be the best.

Alcott, with her freckled face, was one of the candid free spirits. She had fun with whatever she did — playing, working at a bakery or just hanging out — but had a sentimental side to her that showed when she talked about family or special people in golf like Dinah Shore.

And, Jan Stephenson, who was best recognized for her sex appeal early in her career, went on to win 13 tournaments including three major championships in this decade – proving that she truly belonged among the tour's top players.

Facing page: *Patty Sheehan holds the record for the most consecutive $200,000 seasons (15).* **Left:** *Amy Alcott won 19 of her 29 career victories during the 1980s.* **Above:** *In 1999, after 26 years on tour, Jan Stephenson recorded her best season earnings of $296,347.*

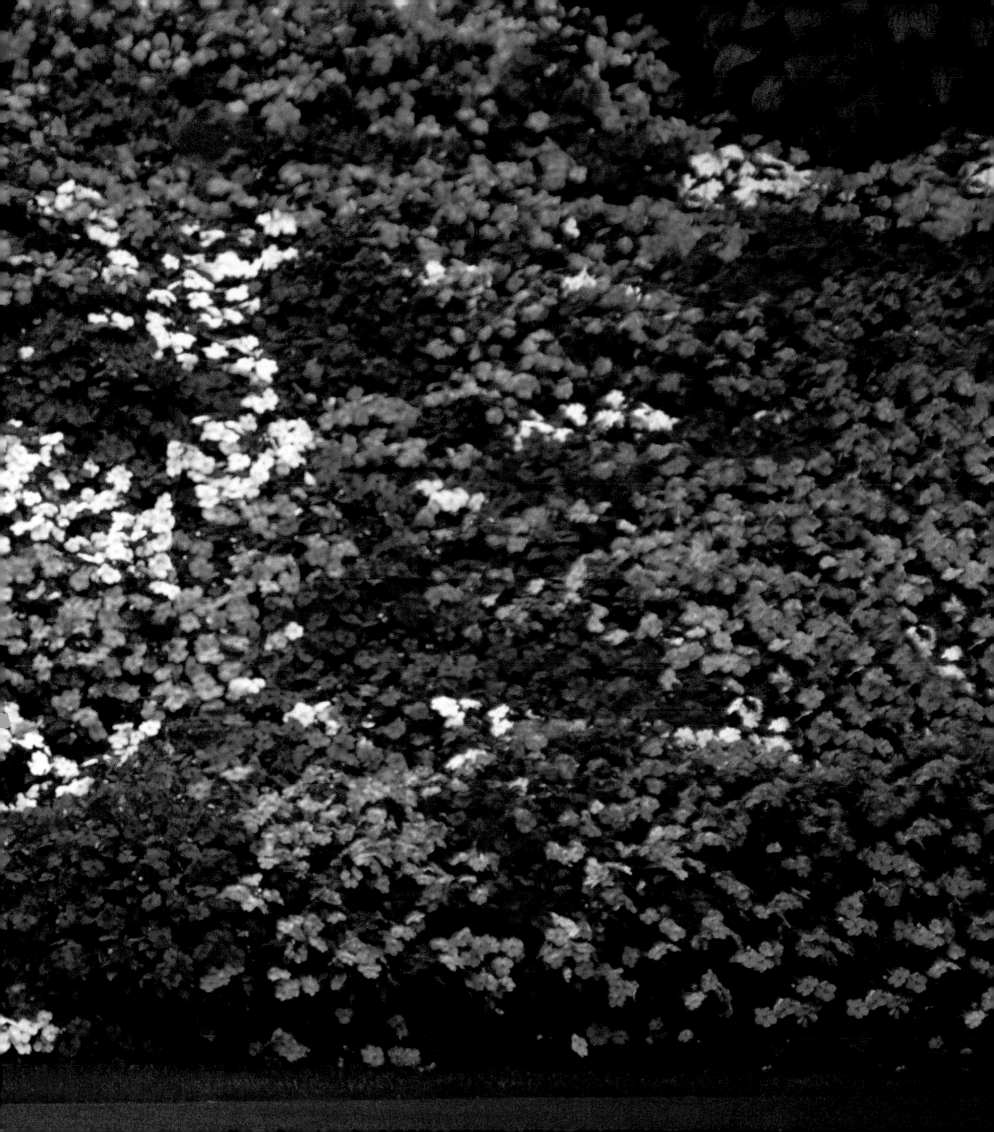

Top left: *In 1999, Rosie Jones recorded her 10th victory and was ranked fourth in putting, with a 29.15 average.* **Bottom left:** *Meg Mallon was ranked as one of the top-10 players for seven years during the 1990s.* **Above:** *Lorie Kane holds the record for the most sub-par rounds in a season with 71 in 1999.* **Facing page:** *The effortless swing of Kelly Robbins produced nine victories, including one major, during her first eight years on the LPGA Tour.*

INTO THE FUTURE

Golf's objective has changed little since its early days when bored Scottish shepherds swatted makeshift balls through pastures with crooked sticks for entertainment.

BY LISA D. MICKEY

But while the equipment, playing fields, swing techniques, clothing, formal organization and scoring prowess of golfers have bounded ahead dramatically over the years, one has to wonder how the game's future will look.

Fifty years from now, how will the LPGA have moved ahead and carved its place in the world of professional golf? How will it influence young women to take up the game, develop their skills and learn to compete? How will it fit into the greater realm of sports and competitive athletics? And, how will its global development shape the future of women's professional golf and continue to build its worldwide audience?

"We're the oldest, most successful women's sports organization in the world," said Ty Votaw, the LPGA's sixth commissioner. "We're the hip grandmother of women's sports and we feel very good about that."

The LPGA boasts two distinct entities: its touring division and its Teaching and Club Professional (T&CP) Division. While the professional tour is the main attraction, the LPGA's T&CP Division, which has 1,100 members, is the association's outreach arm. They are the teachers in communities throughout America who offer clinics and lessons. They are the club professionals who help amateur golfers select equipment and apparel. And they are the coaches and golf industry professionals who make key decisions about the game on various levels.

"They are our voice on the grassroots level and they are the champions of the LPGA out in the field," said Karen Durkin, LPGA vice president of marketing.

Facing page: *As one of the winningest rookies in LPGA history, South Korean Se Ri Pak's future success appears definite.*
Above: *Building for the future, junior tournaments allow girls to test their competitive playing skills.*

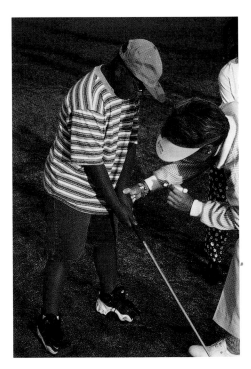

"Bring the club up real slow; bring it up real high; extend your arms real far; hit the ball right on the sweet spot and send it into the middle of the fairway. Then keep hitting it until it's in the hole."

Domingo Lopez' advice to daughter, Nancy.

Certainly, the lifeblood of the LPGA has always been its focus to include, rather than to exclude potential golfers from all backgrounds. Initiatives such as the LPGA's Teacher Education Program for Accessible Golf and the Urban Youth Program make golf possible for many who would otherwise not have access to the training facilities. While the Accessible Golf program trains golf, health and education professionals how to teach golf to individuals with physical limitations, the Urban Youth program strives to introduce golf to inner-city boys and girls, ages 7 to 17. Typically, 80 percent of the Urban Youth program's 1,850 participants are African-American or Hispanic. With the help of corporate sponsorship they receive not only instruction, but equipment and clothing which helps them better adapt to the game. "The LPGA's entire philosophy is geared to the individual and focuses on what they can do, not what they can't do," says Donna White, an LPGA teaching pro and member of the tour for 15 years.

Many of the LPGA outreach teaching programs have benefited from the success of the professional tour. Young athletes, who would have never considered golf, as well as junior golfers, who learned the game from family members, have had their pre-existing ideas about the game changed in recent years due to the youthful star power of such players as Tiger Woods and Annika Sorenstam. Suddenly, for many youngsters, golf has become something more than an adult pastime. In fact, 2,500 girls across America have enrolled in the LPGA's Girls Golf Club junior developmental program. Partnered with the U.S. Golf Association and the Girl Scouts of the USA, the program offers structured golf activities to encourage girls ages 7 to 17 to play.

Facing page: Learning to play golf is a brand-new experience for many children. Teaching pros and clinics can bring golf to life for young players of all ability levels. **Right:** *The key to making golf appeal to youngsters is to make it fun.*

"Golf is just a wonderful game. I never get tired of playing golf, thinking about golf or working with it." Betsy Rawls

But the LPGA's outreach doesn't stop there. At regular tour stops, LPGA playing pros, as well as members of the LPGA's T&CP Division, offer LPGA Tour Junior Golf Clinics to any children large enough to take a swing at a ball. On the other end of the spectrum are the LPGA Golf Clinics for Women held in cities across America to teach women in business the game.

These programs are reinforced by The LPGA Foundation, which was established in 1991. Funds from the foundation support junior golf, academic scholarships for junior golfers and provide emergency financial assistance to those in need within the world of golf.

For certain, the LPGA has invested deeply in its future to make sure that the next generation of players gets off to a solid start. Its programs assure that youngsters from all ethnic, economic and geographic backgrounds can have ample opportunities to develop their skills to enjoy golf, as well as to better understand and appreciate the LPGA. "We have never lost our vision or our focus for golf education or our tenet of bringing more people into the game," says Dr. Betsy Clark, director of education for the LPGA.

Left: *Swing clinics, such as this one at the du Maurier Classic, offer structured fun.* **Above:** *Kay McMahon (right), former president of the LPGA T&CP Division, demonstrates a grip adjustment to a student.* **Facing page:** *LPGA memorabilia, including the first LPGA teaching manual and a picture of Marilynn Smith giving instructions to a junior player, reflect the importance of its teaching division.*

INTO THE FUTURE

"Golf takes a lot of blood and sweat. It's like a great pianist once said, 'If I don't practice one day, I will know it; if I don't practice the second day, my instructor will know it; if I don't practice the third day, the whole world will know it.'" Alice Bauer

While the LPGA's T&CP Division is doing its part to help grow the game, the tournament division also is having an impact. Each year, more players from pro tours in Europe, Asia and Australia show up at the qualifying school in hopes of becoming LPGA touring professionals. The LPGA Tour is the ultimate goal of many international players who opt to come to America to play collegiate golf, familiarize themselves with American culture and geography and improve their skills in the English language. The next obvious step for aspiring pros is the LPGA Tour. Some earn tour cards at the qualifying school, while others compete in the LPGA's developmental Futures Tour before moving on to the LPGA.

The future likely will feature tournament fields more reflective of the world's ethnic and racial composition. As more African-Americans enter the game, and as more Asian and Latin-American players join pro tours, organizations like the LPGA Tour will showcase their own culturally diverse membership. LaRee Pearl Sugg regained her tour card in 2000 to join the LPGA Tour as only the third black player in the tour's history (behind Althea Gibson and Renée Powell). Others are sure to follow.

"I never look at it as a burden," said Sugg, who played at UCLA. "It's a chance for me to inspire people and give people hope."

Facing page: *Many LPGA players participate in teaching clinics at the tour's tournaments. Golfers of all ages relish the chance to work with a tour player during these clinics.* **Right:** *LaRee Sugg is the third African-American professional to compete on the LPGA Tour.*

As the reputation of the LPGA grows, it attracts more and more international talent. **Above:** Grace Park was the top-ranked player in the 1999 SBC Futures Tour before joining the LPGA Tour in 2000. **Facing page:** Akiko Fukushima won two tournaments during her 1999 rookie year.

Long before the public outcry in 1990 at Shoal Creek when the PGA Championship was played at a club that did not welcome black golfers, the LPGA had taken its own stand against discriminatory membership practices at host clubs for LPGA Tour stops. The LPGA has held firm in its position not to play at clubs that impose racially restrictive practices, and in past years its members vetoed tournament sponsors' attempts to hold "invitationals."

"I know the LPGA actually dropped a few events because some clubs didn't want all of our members to play," said Judy Dickinson, who joined the tour in 1978 and has become a student of LPGA history. "That's a strong stand when you have sponsors wanting to hold an event but trying to tell you who can play in it. I think that took a lot of guts by the LPGA, and the players supported the tour's policy."

While Nancy Lopez was the first highly successful player of Hispanic background, others, such as Mexican teen Lorena Ochoa, Colombian sisters Cristina and Marisa Baena and Brazil's Candy Hannemann, will likely make their own impact in women's professional golf. Pacific Rim influence already has broadened the LPGA's global mix. Players such as Japan's Ayako Okamoto (of the 1980s), South Korean Se Ri Pak (beginning in the late 1990s) and 1999 Rookie of the Year Mi Hyun Kim of Korea have led the way for other Asian players to come to America to play the world's top women's tour. Next in line will be Korean Grace Park, Filipinos Dorothy Delasin and Jenny Rosales, as well as sure-bet future pros Jimin Kang of Korea, Candie Kung of Taiwan, and twin sisters of Thailand/Korea Aree Song and Naree Song Wongluekiet, who already have shattered numerous U.S. junior amateur records.

"After I won, I went back to my country.

I tried to wear different clothes and go shopping, but still,

they knew me. Pretty amazing." Se Ri Pak

Ironically, one of the LPGA's biggest challenges in the long run may come in its attempt to attract more American girls to golf and help them move into the professional ranks. Top American prospects, such as Kellee Booth (an LPGA rookie in 2000), Jenna Daniels, Beth Bauer, Leigh Anne Hardin and Natalie Gulbis (who was medalist at age 16 of the stroke-play portion of the 1999 U.S. Women's Amateur), will have their work cut out for them on the tour as their golf careers advance to the professional level. Europeans, Australians, and in recent years, Asians and Canadians, have consistently offered American pros their toughest competition on the LPGA Tour. In the

1990s, only two Americans – Brandie Burton (1991) and Pat Hurst (1995) – won LPGA rookie-of-the-year honors. The award went to international players in the other eight years of that decade, indicating the strength of foreign players. By setting up its numerous developmental programs, the LPGA hopes enough home-grown youngsters will aspire to play on the American-based "world tour" of the LPGA.

"Girls in the United States have many more options in the activities they choose," said Votaw. "We constantly ask ourselves, 'Are we a world tour based in the U.S., or are we an American tour with a number of international players?' "

As increasing numbers of players from around the globe pursue a spot on the LPGA Tour, the American players welcome the opportunity to compete against the world's best. **Left:** *Sweden's Charlotta Sorenstam joined her sister, Annika, as a member of the tour in 1997.* **Facing page:** *In 1993, during her third year on the tour, Brandie Burton became the youngest player to cross the $1 million mark in career earnings.*

INTO THE FUTURE

"We have 50 years of history, and a foundation on which to build. The LPGA Tour has stood the test of time." Ty Votaw, LPGA Commissioner

As golf changes, so do attitudes about golf as a sport for youngsters. This generation of girls is growing up in athletics, so their understanding of competition is greater than young women of previous decades. Sports are no longer viewed solely for boys and golf no longer is seen only as a sport for elderly recreation, thanks to avid players such as former NBA star Michael Jordan. Young pro stars, such as Woods, Karrie Webb, Sorenstam, Pak, Sergio Garcia and Casey Martin, have caused kids throughout the world to take notice of an old game with new appeal. The end result for the LPGA is that women are becoming more avid players, as well as fans, of many sports — including golf. And today's top players have had the benefits of improved coaching, equipment, practice facilities, golf courses and school budgets for women's golf, which makes them better prepared as they move into the professional ranks.

And as the best players in the world continue to come to America to play professional golf, those top players will impact the tour in many ways. They already have recorded new low-season scoring averages, helped lower tournament field 36-hole cuts and carded new all-time low scores at weekly 72-hole events. They can now airmail drives 300 yards down the fairway, spin approach shots on the green and challenge the game's all-time low scores on a regular basis. They also now have unprecedented earning power, which is sure to grow as television coverage expands globally.

"I'm excited and impatient regarding what opportunities lie ahead for us," said Votaw. Clearly, those opportunities are many and varied. And it's evident the LPGA's future is now, unfolding like a giant passport to a sparkling tour of talent from across the globe.

Facing page: *In 1999, Canadian Lorie Kane competed in the first Nation's Cup tournament, which pits top U.S. LPGA players against the top Canadians. Ranked fifth on the season-ending money list in 1999, Kane is one of the tour's great ambassadors.*
Right: *With one win and six top-10 finishes in her second year on tour, Kelli Kuehne is one of the United States' bright young stars.*

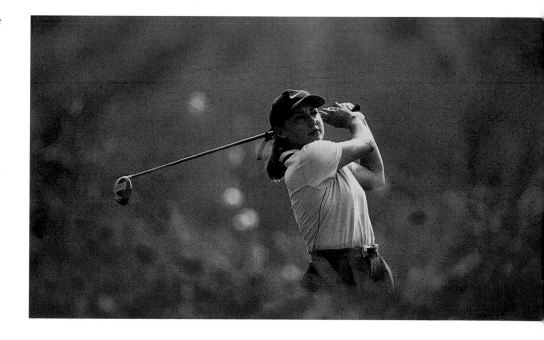

Newcomers to the LPGA
Tour within the last decade
have hailed from all parts of
the world. **Top, left:** *Lisa
Hackney, Great Britain;*
right: *Mi Hyun Kim, South
Korea.* **Bottom, left:** *Mayumi
Hirase, Japan;* **right:** *Maria
Hjorth, Sweden.*
Facing page: *Marnie
McGuire, New Zealand.*

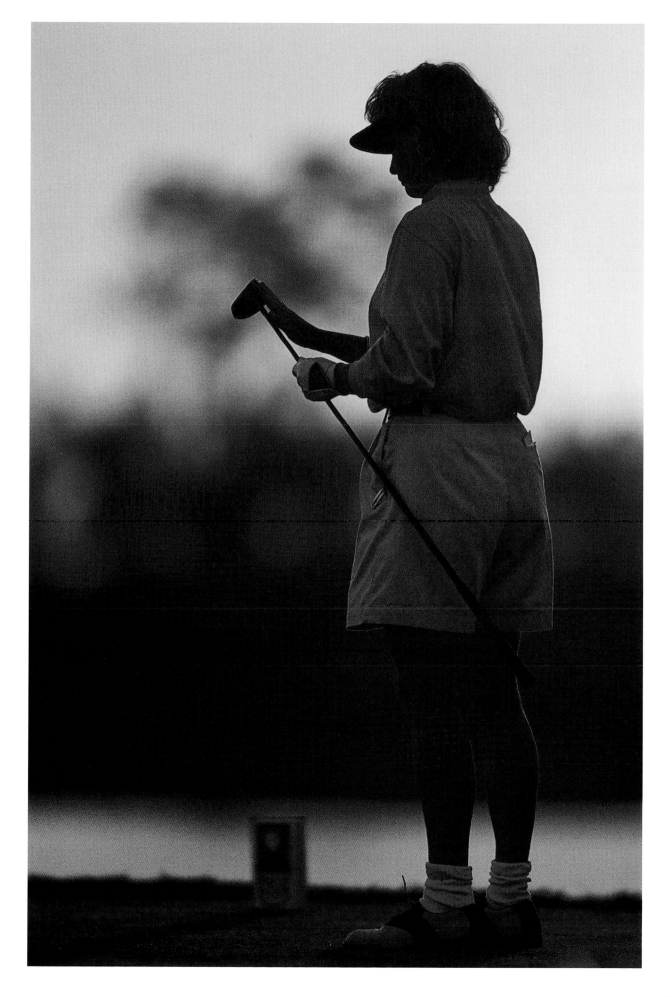

INTO THE FUTURE

The LPGA Tour has been called the "world tour" for a reason. The curtural diversity of its members reflects the growing universal appeal of the sport.

Facing page: *Annika Sorenstam has been so successful on the tour that by early 2000 she had earned enough points to qualify for the LPGA Tour Hall of Fame.*

Above, left: *Pearl Sinn was a Rolex First-Time Winner in 1998, winning the State Farm Rail Classic;* **right:** *Emilee Klein had a successful amateur record, but no professional playing experience before joining the LPGA Tour.*

Top European players have a chance to compete against top American players every two years in the Solheim Cup, a goal for many LPGA members such as Carin Koch **(above)** *of Sweden and Trish Johnson* **(facing page)** *of Great Britain.*

Above: *Cindy Flom has five career victories.* **Top right:** *Sherri Steinhauer celebrates her 1998 Weetabix Women's British Open win.* **Bottom right:** *Barb Mucha's five tournament wins include a 2-0 playoff record.*

The will to win and the pursuit of perfection is the same for all players from veterans to rookies, from the young to the seasoned. Regardless of where they are from, they all share the goal of making their mark in golf. Each member of the LPGA, whether touring pro or teacher, contributes to making it what it is and what it will become. **Top left:** *Aree Song Wongluekiet, 13, and her twin sister Naree Song, are the youngest players ever to be invited to compete in an LPGA event.* **Top right:** *Japan's Riko Higashio at the 1999 LPGA Qualifier.* **Bottom right:** *Canadian A.J. Eathorne recorded three top-10 finishes during her 1999 rookie year.*

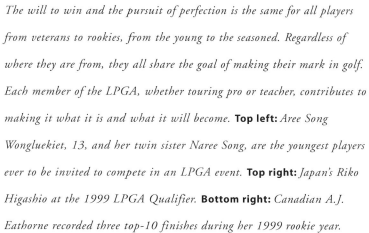

THE RECORD BREAKERS

No one won more often. Not even Jack Nicklaus or Sam Snead. And, maybe not even Tiger Woods. Eighty-eight wins. They came during a 24-year window and defined an incredible 33-year career that spilled into five decades.

BY MELANIE HAUSER

They brought a record eight money titles, a record seven Player of the Year awards, a record seven Vare Trophies and three stints as LPGA president. The owner of those 88 titles and a few other records is Kathrynne Ann Whitworth. The incomparable Kathy with that unflappable bouffant hairdo and unbelievable resilience. The lanky young Kathy who finished near the bottom of the list in her pro debut, but got the last laugh. The Hall-of-Famer Kathy, whose 88 LPGA wins are the most by any golf professional — man or woman — ever.

Whitworth started the list with a win at the 1962 Kelly Girl Open and added one final exclamation point of a win at the 1985 United Virginia Bank Classic. And along the way? Well, in 1982 she won No. 83 and flew past Mickey Wright, who holds the record for most tournaments won in a season with 13 in 1963. Whit then bested Snead, who has 81 PGA Tour wins, with her victory in the Rochester International in 1984. She became the first woman to win $1 million too, reaching that goal in 1981, and she set records for consecutive seasons with at least one win (17) and the most seasons with a win (22). She also holds the record for most aces in a career with 11. Yet as amazing as Whitworth's marks are, they're not the only ones that grab your attention.

Take Pat Bradley and Juli Inkster. They're the only two women to win all four modern majors. Bradley did it first, winning three majors, including the final two to her slam in 1986, while Inkster played her way into the record books and the Hall of Fame, winning two majors to complete her slam in 1999. Mickey Wright and Louise Suggs were the only two players to win the four early-era major championships. Suggs accomplished it in 1957, followed by Wright in 1962. Or how about Patty Berg, who won a record 15 majors? Or Judy Rankin, who set a standard in 1973 with 25 top-10 finishes?

*Facing page: Kathy Whitworth is not only the winningest golfer in history, but over the years has been an active contributor to the growth of the LPGA and the game of golf. **Above:** Pat Bradley, the first player to win the modern Grand Slam, displays trophies from her four majors.*

The growth and popularity of women's professional and amateur golf has been significantly influenced by the efforts and activities of the LPGA. There have been many extraordinary people who have been a part of its history and success, including those shown on these pages. Built upon a foundation of indomitable spirit, unwavering determination and tremendous talent, the future of the LPGA promises to be exciting for player and public alike.

Top, left: *Three-time Nabisco Dinah Shore winner Amy Alcott with Dinah Shore, who was often called "the first lady of women's golf";* **right:** *Karsten and Louise Solheim with Judy Rankin, winner of two Solheim Cups, as captain of the U.S. team.* **Bottom:** *Charlie Mechem, former LPGA Commissioner, and Helen Alfredsson.*

Facing page, top left: *Babe Zaharias led the crusade for women's golf in the early years;* **top right:** *Public support for the LPGA tournaments and media coverage of its events continues to grow each year;* **bottom left:** *As LPGA Tournament Director for more than 15 years, Suzanne Jackson was considered a "master" in her field and an expert on the rules of golf;* **bottom right:** *LPGA legends Kathy Whitworth (right) and Mickey Wright teamed up in a rare modern-day appearance at the Sprint Senior Challenge.*

CREATIVE CONTRIBUTORS

MELANIE HAUSER, *Author (text), Houston, TX*
Melanie is an award-winning freelance columnist and feature writer, who has covered the LPGA Tour and the PGA Tour for the past 24 years. She currently serves as secretary-treasurer of the Golf Writers Association of America. She is author of *Under the Lone Star Flagstick, A Collection of Writings on Texas Golf and Golfers*, published by Simon & Schuster.

LIZ KAHN, *Author (text), Hertfordshire, England*
A journalist and sports writer, Liz has been a regular contributor to British and international newspapers and magazines. She participated in the founding of the Women's PGA in Europe and was the first woman member and woman captain of the Press Golfing Society in Britain. Liz has authored two books, *The LPGA, The Unauthorized Version* and *Tony Jacklin, The Price of Success*.

LISA D. MICKEY, *Author (text and captions), Bridgeport, CT*
As an editor at *Golf World* magazine, Lisa covers the LPGA, NCAA, amateur golf and golf equipment. She is a frequent contributor to *Golf Digest* and is the Equipment Editor for *Golf Digest Woman* magazine. Previously, Lisa spent four years at *Golf for Women* as a senior editor and worked as a sportswriter for newspapers in North Carolina. She is a Women's Sports Foundation national journalism award winner.

NANETTE S. SANSON, *Author (captions)/Photo and Text Editor/Art Director, Toronto, Ontario*
For more than 20 years, Nanette has been immersed in the field of visual communications as a photographer, an owner of a stock photo agency for 13 years, and since 1994, the owner of Profolio Editions Inc. of Naples, FL, a publisher of specialty picture books. Her previous book, *In Portrait: NAPLES and Collier County*, was an international award winner.

SANDI HIGGS, *Text Editor/Author (captions), Port Hope, FL*
Sandi has been a member of the LPGA staff since 1986. She served as Media Services Coordinator and Manager of Broadcast Services before assuming her current position as Manager of Online Services.

JULIE G. MARVEL, *Text Editor, Cheshire, CT*
Julie has 15 years of experience in the sports communication field and was actively involved with the LPGA in the late 1980s as Director of Communications. She then spent eight seasons with the NBA's Golden State Warriors and two years at FirstTour Junior Golf as Director of Communications.

MELISSA YOW, *Copy Editor, Bridgeport, CT*
Melissa is the copy editor of *Golf Digest* and *Golf Digest Woman* magazines. She spent five years at *Golf for Women* as a senior editor after earning a master's degree in English literature from the University of Mississippi.

DEBORAH A. LEVINSON, *Assistant Photo Editor, Great Barrington, MA*
As a marketing professional and photo editor for more than 25 years, Deborah has focused her career in the advertising, fine art and publishing industries. Following 17 years in the stock photo industry and three years as owner of a fine art gallery, she joined the staff of QuailMark Books as sales manager.

LANDGRAFF DESIGN ASSOCIATES LTD., *Design of Jacket and Interior, Mississauga, Ontario*
For more than 25 years, the creative team at Landgraff Design has been striving for excellence in the graphic design field, specializing in the design of books, identities and corporate literature under the art direction of Michael Landgraff.

BERGMAN GRAPHICS, *Prepress, Colchester, VT*
Bergmans serves the graphic arts industry with a wide range of digital solutions including photography, prepress services, asset management and direct-to-plate printing, from locations in Vermont and New Hampshire. For this project, Bergmans supplied all color separations, custom color tinting, proofing services and final film output.

PHOTOGRAPHY CREDITS

ALLSPORT

> **SIMON BRUTY** pg: 25 (top left)
>
> **J.D. CUBAN** pg: 8-9, 54 (top right)
>
> **STEPHEN DUNN** pg: 59 (bottom right)
>
> **HARRY HOW** pg: cover inset (Sorenstam), 35, 62 (top right), 63, 70-71, 87 (top left), 110 (top left), 139, 140 (bottom left)
>
> **CRAIG JONES** pg: 7
>
> **DONALD MIRALLE** pg: 54 (bottom left), 79, 104-105, 135, 144
>
> **STEPHEN MUNDAY** pg: 146 (top)
>
> **MIKE POWELL** pg: 128 (top)
>
> **ANDREW REDDINGTON** pg: 33 (top right), 78 (left), 114-115, 143 (left)
>
> **JAMIE SQUIRE** pg: 54 (top left)

AP/WIDE WORLD PHOTOS pg: 5, 22 (bottom left), 28, 30 (right), 46, 53, 57 (top), 97, 107 (top left), 147 (top left), 152 (top left)

B. PROUD PHOTOGRAPHY pg: 60 (top left), 61 (top left), 61 (top right), 124 (top left), 128 (bottom center), 129, 142, 143 (right),

DIANE BELANGER/PROFOLIO pg: 10, 11, 17, 39, 131, back cover.

FRED BOURDON pg: 61 (bottom)

CORBIS/BETTEMANN pg: cover inset (Babe Zaharias) and 4, 19 (top), 21, cover inset (Mickey Wright) and 22 (right), 30 (center), 40 (top center), 41 (left center), 41 (top left), 47 (left), 54 (top center), 54 (bottom center), 98 (top left), 150

DEE DARDEN pg: 2, 12, 24, 31, 33 (top right), 34 (top center), 34 (left), 34 (bottom center), 49, 50 (left), 50 (right), 52 (top left), 67 (bottom), 68 (bottom right), 73, 83 (center), 83 (right), 89, 106, 109 (right), 110 (bottom left), 111, 112, 113 (all), 117, 121, 124 (bottom left), 136, 140 (top left), 145, 146 (bottom left), 151 (top left), 152 (bottom left), 153 (bottom left)

MARTY DEDRICK/STOPACTION PHOTOS pg: 52 (bottom)

DU MAURIER CLASSIC pg: 32 (bottom right), 87 (top right), 146 (bottom right)

BOB EWELL pg: 54 (left center), 60 (bottom left), 77 (bottom), 87 (bottom right), 107 (bottom left), 109 (left), 116 (top left), 125, 137, 156

PETE FONTAINE/SPORTIMAGE pg: 62 (bottom left), 74 (top)

KEVIN FRAYER/CN PRESS pg: 138, 147 (bottom right)

MARC GLASSMAN pg: 52 (top right)

GOLF DIGEST pg: 20, 103

> **STEPHEN SZURLEJ** pg: 81 (bottom left), 116 (top right)

GOLF WORLD pg: 40 (top right), 41 (top center), 41 (bottom center), 41 (bottom right), 45 (top), 47 (right) and cover inset (Kathy Whitworth), 56, 77 (top), 96

ROB GRIFFIN pg: 25 (bottom left), 68 (top right), 122-123, 151 (bottom right)

KIM HIGGINS pg: 1, 3, 13, 25 (right), 26-27, 33 (bottom left), 51, 54 (bottom right), 66, 67 (top), 68 (top left), 69 (all), 85, 86, 107 (bottom right), 116 (bottom left), 118, 119, 120, 124 (top right), 126, 140 (top right), 141, 147 (top right)

JEFF HORNBACK pg: 37, 54 (center), 54 (right center), 59 (bottom left), 72 (bottom left), 107 (top right)

LEONARD KAMSLER pg: 48 (top left), 98 (right), 110 (right), 149

THE LPGA pg: 15, 16, 30 (left), 32 (bottom left), 38 (top), 40 (bottom center), 80, 84, 90

RALPH W. MILLER GOLF LIBRARY pg: 32 (top right), 40 (center), 40 (bottom right), 92 (top), 98 (bottom left)

ELIZABETH OPALENIK pg: 57 (bottom), 68 (bottom left), 82, 132, 152 (top right)

K. PATTERSON/ATLANTA JOURNAL CONSTITUTION pg: 29

LEW PORTNOY/LPPHOTO.COM pg: 32 (top left), 34 (right), 48 (bottom left), 94, 99, 100, 101, 102, 148

RAY REISS pg: 60 (top right)

ROBERT REYNOLDS pg: 58

RICK SHARP pg: 6, 33 (bottom right), 42, 55, 72 (top left), 72 (bottom right), 74 (bottom), 75 (top right), 75 (center), 81 (top left), 81 (bottom right), 83 (left), 88, 108, 116 (bottom right), 127, 128 (bottom right), 130 (top), 133, 134, 140 (bottom right), 153 (top right), 153 (bottom right)

SPORTS ILLUSTRATED

> **JIM GUND** pg: 91
>
> **RICHARD MACKSON** pg: 22 (top left), 48 (right)
>
> **G. ROSSI** pg: 72 (top right)

JACK STOHLMAN pg: 36, 59 (top left), 75 (top left), 81 (top right), 128 (bottom left)

USGA pg: 18, 19 (bottom), 40 (top left), 40 (bottom left), 41 (top right), 44 (left), 44 (right), 92 (bottom left), 92 (bottom right), 93, 95, 153 (top left)

DON VICKERY pg: 64 (all), 65 (all), 75 (bottom left), 78 (top), 130 (bottom), 151 (top right)

FRED VUICH/GOLF MAGAZINE pg: cover inset (Nancy Lopez)

ROBERT WALKER pg: 38 (bottom), 62 (top left), 75 (bottom right)

WILSON SPORTS pg: 45 (bottom) and cover (background)

WORLD GOLF VILLAGE pg: 43